Shinto

Titles in the Religions of the World series include:

Buddhism
Confucianism
Hinduism
Islam
Shinto

Shinto

Stuart A. Kallen

Lucent Books, Inc.
10911 Technology Place, San Diego, California, 92127

Library of Congress Cataloging-in-Publication Data

Kallen, Stuart A., 1955–
    Shinto / by Stuart A. Kallen.
        p. cm. — (Religions of the world)
Summary: Discusses historical origins, the teachings, practices, spread
of Shinto into modern times.
Includes bibliographical references and index.
    ISBN 1-56006-988-0
1. Shinto. I. Title. II Religions of the world (San Diego, Calif.)
BL2220 .K276 2002
299'.561—dc21

2001006120

Printed in the U.S.A.

Contents

Foreword

Religion has always been a central component of human culture, though its form and practice have changed through time. Ancient people lived in a world they could not explain or comprehend. Their world consisted of an environment controlled by vague and mysterious powers attributed to a wide array of gods. Artifacts dating to a time before recorded history suggest that the religion of the distant past reflected this world, consisting mainly of rituals devised to influence events under the control of these gods.

The steady advancement of human societies brought about changes in religion as in all other things. Through time, religion came to be seen as a system of beliefs and practices that gave meaning to—or allowed acceptance of—anything that transcended the natural or the known. And, the belief in many gods ultimately was replaced in many cultures by the belief in a Supreme Being.

As in the distant past, however, religion still provides answers to timeless questions: How, why, and by whom was the universe created? What is the ultimate meaning of human life? Why is life inevitably followed by death? Does the human soul continue to exist after death, and if so, in what form? Why is there pain and suffering in the world, and why is there evil?

In addition, all the major world religions provide their followers with a concrete and clearly stated ethical code. They offer a set of moral instructions, defining virtue and evil and what is required to achieve goodness. One of these universal moral codes is compassion toward others above all else. Thus, Judaism, Christianity, Islam, Hinduism, Buddhism, Confucianism, and Taoism each teach a version of the so-called golden rule, or in the words of Jesus Christ, "As ye would that men should do to you, do ye also to them likewise." (Luke 6:31) For example, Confucius instructed his disciples to "never impose on others what you would not choose for yourself." (*Analects* : 12:2) The Hindu epic poem, Mahabarata, identifies the core of all Hindu teaching as not doing unto others what you do not wish done to yourself, and Muhammad declared that no Muslim could be a true believer unless he desired for his brother no less than that which he desires for himself.

It is ironic, then, that although compassionate concern for others forms the heart of all the major religions' moral teachings, religion has also been at the root of countless conflicts throughout history. It has been suggested that much of the appeal that religions hold for humankind lies in their unswerving faith in the truth of their particular vision. Throughout history, most religions have shared a profound confidence that their interpretation of life, God, and the universe is the right one, thus giving their followers a sense of certainty in an uncertain and often fragile existence. Given the assurance displayed by most religions regarding the fundamental correctness of their teachings and practices, it is perhaps not surprising that religious intolerance has fueled disputes and even full-scale wars between peoples and nations time and time again, from the Crusades of medieval times to the current bloodshed in Northern Ireland and the Middle East.

Today, as violent religious conflicts trouble many parts of our world, it has become more important than ever to learn about the similarities as well as the differences between faiths. One of the most effective ways to accomplish this is by examining the beliefs, customs, and values of various religions. In the Religions of the World series, students will find a clear description of the core creeds, rituals, ethical teachings, and sacred texts of the world's major religions. In-depth explorations of how these faiths changed over time, how they have influenced the social customs, laws, and education of the countries in which they are practiced, and the particular challenges each one faces in coming years are also featured.

Extensive quotations from primary source materials, especially the core scriptures of each faith, and a generous number of secondary source quotations from the works of respected modern scholars are included in each volume in the series. It is hoped that by gaining insight into the faiths of other peoples and nations, students will not only gain a deeper appreciation and respect for different religious beliefs and practices, but will also gain new perspectives on and understanding of their own religious traditions.

The Shinto Religion

Shinto is the native religion of Japan. It has been practiced by the Japanese people since about 500 B.C. and continues to influence nearly every facet of life on that island nation.

The Shinto belief system is based on a reverence of nature, the veneration of family and ancestors, and the desire to honor gods, goddesses, and sacred spirits.

Shinto is an animist belief system, meaning that it attributes mystical powers to natural objects such as mountains, rivers, waterfalls, trees, lightning, the sun, some animals, and ancestral spirits. Shinto practitioners believe that there are more than 8 million of these sacred deities called *kami* and that they permeate all aspects of human existence. Gorazd Vihar and Charlotte Anderson explain this concept in *Matsuri: World of Japanese Festivals:*

> It is believed that the world functions through the cooperation of the *kami* . . . and strives toward the social harmony in which the gods rejoice. The kami are linked inextricably to the Japanese psyche, so much so that it has been said that without Japan there would be no Shinto, and without Shinto, no Japan.[1]

Of the 128 million people in Japan, about 110 million practice Shinto. At least three-quarters of the Japanese people also practice Buddhism, a complex religion that consists of the teachings of the Buddha, Siddhartha Gautama, which originated in India in the sixth century A.D.

When Buddhism was first introduced to Japan, it was resisted by some, but soon a great many people were practicing both religions. According to the Religious Tolerance website: "Within Shinto, the Buddha

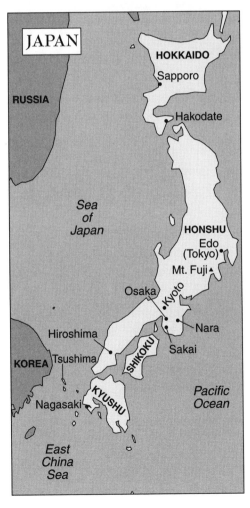

JAPAN

was viewed as another *kami* (nature deity). Meanwhile, Buddhism in Japan regarded the *Kami* as being manifestations of various Buddhas."[2] As such, Buddhism and Shinto complement each other, and today a large majority of Japanese people observe both religions.

Although Buddhism is commonly practiced in Japan, it is the dedication to Shinto that has shaped the Japanese culture. As C. Scott Littleton writes in *Eastern Wisdom:*

> Such ubiquitous customs as the daily bath and removing one's shoes before entering a home have roots in Shinto's pervasive concern with purification, and the reverence shown by the Japanese towards nature stems from the Shinto belief that spirit-beings *[kami]* occupy and govern the natural world.[3]

The Japanese Environment

It is little wonder that a religion dedicated to nature developed in the beautiful environment found in Japan. The country itself is made up of four large islands, and over a thousand smaller ones, situated on the western edge of what is known as the Ring of Fire—a continuous belt containing 75 percent of the

Japan's landscape is dotted with 188 volcanoes, including the dormant Mount Fuji (pictured).

world's volcanoes that stretches from the Americas to Asia. This zone is notorious for frequent earthquakes and volcanic eruptions. What this means for Japan is nearly constant seismic activity, punctuated by often devastating earthquakes.

Japan has 188 volcanoes, sixty of which are active. These volcanoes have created mountains over time, and these mountains dominate Japan's landscape. When not blocked by clouds and air pollution, the shimmering snowcapped peak of Mount Fuji, a dormant volcano, can be seen towering nearly 12,400 feet above sea level. Because Japan has very little flat land, much of the country is not suitable for building. As a result, most people live in major cities, of which Tokyo is the largest, with almost one-quarter of the nation's population.

While cities like Tokyo consist of concrete urban landscapes, more than 67 percent of the country is still covered with forests, and the climate ranges from semitropical in the south to bitter cold in the north. In between there are mountain ranges, lakes, hot springs, fast-running rivers, waterfalls, and a wide variety of flora and fauna. It is here, among nature, where the Japanese people believe that the *kami* are most abundant.

A Spirit of Cooperation

Although Japan is also one of the most densely populated nations in the world, its people work together in an unparalleled spirit of cooperation that can be traced to the Shinto religion. Since the Japanese believe that every person and everything is born of *kami*, then every person is deserving of the respect afforded to the gods. This feeling also unites the Japanese people in a common bond. As Beth Reiber writes in *Tokyo:*

> The Japanese feel that they belong to one huge tribe different from any other people on earth.
>
> While in the West the recipe for a full and rewarding life seems to be in that elusive attainment of "happiness," in Japan it's the satisfactory performance of duty and obligation. While in the West individuality is encouraged and nurtured, in Japan individuality is equated with selfishness and a complete disregard for the feelings and consideration of others. The Japanese are instilled with a sense of duty toward the group—whether it be family, friends, coworkers, or Japanese society as a whole—so that consideration of the group always wins over the desires of the individual.[4]

Living in cooperation with each other and the ancient *kami* spirits, the people of Japan have built one of the most advanced civilizations the world has ever known. Jean Herbert, author of *Shinto: At the Fountainhead of Japan,* believes that Shinto

> has been a factor in the moulding of the Japanese [people], not only in their religious outlook and activities, but also in their social patterns and their individual behaviour, in their ethics and their mental attitude towards life. From it arises respect for all that is . . . a high sense of duty, and a feeling of security and . . . fearlessness.[5]

Today people in Japan's gleaming modern cities continue to blend ancient cultural beliefs with the demands of modern society. With their roots deep in the ageless Shinto system, they make their way in the world with one foot planted in the twenty-first century and the other firmly rooted in the ancient magic of the *kami* way.

chapter one

The Historic Roots of Shinto

The roots of Shinto are as old as the Japanese people themselves. Piecing together archaeological evidence, researchers believe that the Japanese began to form a civilization around the eighth century B.C. The first period of that civilization, the Jomon, or Neolithic Age, lasted until 250 B.C. The aboriginal people of the Jomon culture, known as the Ainu, used stone tools, such as axes, knives, arrows, and spears, and survived by hunting and fishing.

The Ainu lived in clans called *uji* that were related by either blood or marriage. Their lives revolved around the circle of seasons as their religious ceremonies celebrated events such as planting, harvesting, and fertility. According to the Religious Tolerance web page, the ancient religion was "an amorphous [formless] mix of nature worship, fertility cults, divination techniques, hero worship, and shamanism."[6]

The Ainu people did not worship a single deity, but innumerable animistic spirits called *kami*. In the eighteenth century, the respected Japanese scholar Motoori Norinaga described the *kami*, which also included the emperors and royal families who ruled Japan:

> Speaking in general . . . it may be said the *kami* signifies, in the first place, the deities of heaven and earth . . . and

also the spirits of the shrines where they are worshipped.

It is hardly necessary to say that it includes human beings. It also includes such objects as birds, beasts, trees, plants, seas, mountains, and so forth. In ancient usage, anything whatsoever which was outside the ordinary, which possessed superior power or which was awe-inspiring was called *kami*. . . . Evil and mysterious things, if they are extra-

An intricately decorated terracotta vase from the Jomon period of Japan's history.

ordinary and dreadful, are called *kami*. It is needless to say that among human beings who are called *kami* the successive generations of sacred [Japanese] emperors are all included. . . . In a lesser degree we find, in the present as well as in ancient times, human beings who are *kami*. Although they may not be accepted [as *kami*] throughout the whole country . . . in each province, each village, and each family there are human beings who are *kami*, each one according to his own proper position.[7]

The Clans and the *Kami*

The *uji* depended on *kami* to bless their lives and bring them good luck and prosperity. Each clan was represented by its own *kami*, and although there was no formal priesthood, the head of each *uji* acted as a high priest who listened to the *kami* spirits and interpreted their words for his clan. The chief also spoke to the *kami*, reciting soothing, poetic ritual prayers, called *norito*. It is believed that these magical *norito* phrases, handed down from father to son, could ensure the goodwill of the deities. One such prayer is recalled by Donald Philippi in *Norito: A New Translation of the Ancient Japanese Ritual Prayers:*

When [the chief priest of the Nakatomi] thus pronounces [solemn ritual words]

The heavenly deities . . . will push open the heavenly rock door,

And pushing with an awesome pushing through the myriad layers of heavenly clouds,

Will hear and receive [these words].

Then the earthly deities . . . will climb up

To the summits of the high mountains and to the

Summits of the low mountains,

And pushing aside the mists of the high mountains

And the mists of the low mountains,

Will hear and receive [these words].[8]

The ancient *norito* were not written down until the eighth century but are believed to have survived in their original form, because the words and phrases were thought to have magical powers only if recited precisely in the traditional manner.

The Yamato Conquest

The clans of the ancient Ainu dominated central Japan until 660 B.C. Then, according to *Nihongi* ("Chronicles of Japan"), written in 720 A.D., a ruler named Jimmu Tenno, of the Yamato clan, drove the Ainu out of central Japan.

This detail from an eighteenth-century scroll depicts the Ainu, the aboriginal people of Japan who created Shinto.

Jimmu became the head Shinto priest of the Japanese people and first emperor of Japan. Since that time, all Japanese people have referred to themselves as the Yamato, and this name has also been applied to the region of central Japan south of Nara.

The earliest members of the Yamato clan probably migrated to Japan from China and Korea, where they were skilled in the use of metal. Fighting with knives, spears, axes, and swords made of iron, the Yamato easily displaced the Ainu people.

Like the Ainu, the Yamato were an agricultural people who grew rice and possessed horses and other domesticated animals such as goats and chickens.

Jimmu himself was worshiped as a *kami* because, as Norinaga writes, "from the standpoint of common people, [emperors] are far-separated, majestic and worthy of reverence."[9]

The guardian *kami* of the Yamato clan was the sun goddess, Amaterasu, who became the supreme heavenly deity of Japan. Jimmu and all his ancestors throughout the centuries—including Japan's current emperor—are believed to be direct descendants of Amaterasu. And all were believed to be able to draw on the sun goddess's incredible cosmic powers.

Chinese Influence

By the end of the fourth century A.D., Yamato was a well-established kingdom that conducted an ongoing cultural and political exchange with nearby China. Soldiers, diplomats, artists, and tradesmen often traveled back and forth between the two countries, and Chinese influence remained strong. During this period of cultural exchange, many products from the highly developed Chinese culture found their way to Japan. In *The Pageant of Japanese History*, Marion May Dilts explains:

Men of Yamato returning to their homes [from China] brought with them all they could of Chinese coins and medicines, personal finery and household furnishings such as silks, mirrors, lacquered boxes and stands, pottery, silver and glassware and writing materials; and many of the [Chinese] who came [to Japan] knew how to make such things themselves. They were familiar with ways of fertilizing the soil to raise better crops, with methods of caring for silkworms to get fine strong silk to color and weave into beautifully patterned cloth. But more important . . . they knew how to read and write and could

The Japanese Royal Family

The imperial family of Japan is the only dynasty in the world to have singly ruled a country for nearly its entire existence, as Ken Watanabe explains on the "Japan and the Imperial Household" website:

"Since the foundation of Japan in about 600 B.C., the Imperial Household of Japan (in Japanese, *Koshitsu*) has [maintained] the unbroken line of . . . Emperors as the only dynasty in Japan for over 2600 years. Therefore, presently, the Imperial Household of Japan is the oldest [ruling] family in the world. . . .

The title *Tenno* or *Sumera-Mikoto* (literally 'heavenly sovereign') was first assumed by Japanese rulers in the sixth or seventh century and has been used by all subsequent Japanese sovereigns. The Japanese imperial institution, the oldest hereditary monarchy in the world, was already in existence when Japan emerged into recorded history. . . . Although the emperor has almost always been regarded as the titular head of the national government, the most striking feature of the office through most of Japanese history has been the tendency to [emphasize] instead the emperor's role as chief priest in the indigenous Japanese religion, Shinto, and to delegate most of the effective powers of government to others.

The Emperor figures centrally in a mythology preserved in the historical chronicles *Kojiki* . . . and *Nihon shoki*. . . . According to these, the Sun Goddess Amaterasu O-Mi-Kami, chief divinity of the Shinto pantheon, bequeathed to her grandson Ninigi no Mikoto a mirror, jewels, and a sword, which he in turn passed on to his descendants, the Emperors of Japan, the first of whom was the Emperor Jimmu.

The Emperor was thought to possess magical powers to propitiate or intercede with divinities. However, because of the awe surrounding his person, it was also considered inappropriate for the Emperor to concern himself with the secular business of government."

keep accounts of taxes and trading arrangements.

Since the [Japanese] islanders themselves had never learned these arts, men who were accomplished in writing and reading . . . were employed as scribes by the most important clan leaders who . . . realized that they would seem greater themselves if they had remarkable men around them. In return for their services, the Korean and Chinese refugees were given lands where they could build homes for their families, and abundant provisions for living. Often they were excused from the taxes of rice and cloth or the forced labor that ordinary Japanese rendered to the clan heads for the use of the land, and often because of their ability they were granted the best government positions and honored with official rank. Under such favorable conditions they increased in number; they prospered and began to play a very important part in building up the Japanese nation.[10]

As the status of the Chinese immigrants increased, so did their numbers. By the sixth century there were at least a hundred thousand Chinese people living in Japan, and by the seventh century nearly 25 percent of Japanese nobility traced their ancestry to either China or Korea.

The Rise of Buddhism

The people from the mainland of Asia brought more than furniture and silks. They also introduced the Japanese to several new religions such as Confucianism, Taoism, and Buddhism.

Confucianism is based on the teachings of Confucius, who lived from 551 to 479 B.C. Its doctrines resemble those of Shinto, honoring compassion, loyalty to family, respect for superiors and for the aged, and high esteem for learning.

Daoism, or Taoism, was influential among the working people of China. Its doctrines state that believers should live in harmony with the universe. Like Shinto, Taoism has many gods that are represented in nature, and some of these were adopted by Shinto practitioners.

While Taoism and Confucianism were popular among Japanese, Buddhism had the largest overall influence on Shinto and the people of Japan. The website Schauwecker's Guide to Japan explains that Buddhism's "central theories are that human life is full of suffering due to worldly desires, illness, death and the loss of loved ones. By getting rid of desires and attachments, one can achieve the state of enlightenment (Nirvana) and escape suffering."[11]

Buddhism officially came to Japan in A.D. 552, when a Korean king sent envoys to the Japanese emperor Kimmei to ask for help in fighting a war. The delegation included scores of Buddhist priests in yellow robes who chanted, burned incense, and bore gifts of prayer books, religious flags, ceremonial umbrellas, and a large copper-and-gold statue of Buddha. According to the *Nihongi* chronicles, these envoys delivered a letter to Emperor Kimmei that recommended he learn Buddhism, saying:

> This doctrine is amongst all doctrines the most excellent.

But it is hard to explain, and hard to comprehend. Even . . . Confucius had not attained to a knowledge of it. This doctrine can create religious merit and retribution without measure and without bounds, and so lead on to a full appreciation of the highest wisdom.[12]

Japanese Written Language

There was no written Japanese language until the sixth century A.D. At that time Japan adapted the Chinese *kanji*, or pictograph alphabet, in order to develop a written language. In such a system, each character represents an entire word, rather than a single letter, as in the English alphabet. In later centuries the Japanese added two more phonetic alphabets, the *hiragana* and *katakana*, to the *kanji*, to form a complex writing system.

Chinese and Japanese use some of the same pictographs, but otherwise there's no similarity between the languages. As such, Chinese and Japanese people may be able to read some of each other's written language, but they cannot speak to one another in a common tongue.

The modern Japanese written language—a combination of *kanji*, *hiragana*, and *katakana*—is probably one of the most complex writing systems in the world.

A Japanese scribe. The Japanese adopted their written language from the Chinese alphabet.

Despite this glowing recommendation, Japan's emperors were wary of Buddhism, fearing that if it was adopted, it might offend the *kami*. Soon afterward a plague of smallpox swept across Japan, confirming those fears. The Buddha statue brought by the envoys was cast into the river, and the shrine where it had been housed was set afire. For the next several decades, the conflict between Shinto and the newly introduced religion continued. Regardless of these conflicts, Buddhism continued to gain in popularity among the privileged classes.

The power of Buddhism was greatly enhanced in A.D. 593, when Prince Shotoku became Japan's acting ruler. Shotoku was so interested in Buddhism that he declared it the official religion of Japan and even learned to read and write so he could further explore the teachings of Buddha. His example encouraged other Japanese leaders to learn to read and write, and since that time Shotoku has been referred to as the Father of Japanese Culture.

The Way of the *Kami*

While Buddhism was establishing itself among Japan's ruling classes, the average peasant continued to practice the Shinto religion. For more than eleven centuries, the stories of the *kami* had been passed on from one generation to the next by word of mouth. The Shinto religion itself did not even have a formal name—it simply existed. But as Buddhism began to dominate Japan, the Chinese written alphabet—another import to the country—gave Shinto a formal name in 682.

The word "Shinto" was written with two Chinese pictographic characters. The first, *shin*, represents *"kami,"* or "divine beings." The second character, *to*, means *"no michi"* or "the way." Together, the characters spell "Shinto"— "The Way of the *Kami.*"

Although it now had a name, Japan's native religion might be remembered inaccurately or eclipsed by Buddhism, the Japanese emperor Temmu feared. Temmu issued a formal decree designed to preserve Shinto legends and beliefs in their pure form. According to *The Sacred Scriptures of the Japanese*, edited by Post Wheeler, Temmu stated:

> I therefore now desire that the annals of the Emperors be taken and recorded and the ancient words examined and certified, inventions stricken out and the truth ascertained, for handing down to future ages.[13]

To complete this arduous task, Temmu consulted a twenty-eight-year-old professional "reciter" named Hiyeda no Arè. According to Wheeler, Arè had such an incredible memory that he could "repeat with his mouth whatsoever his eyes saw, and remember in his heart whatsoever struck his ears."[14] Arè was ordered to memorize the genealogy of the imperial family and the ancient wisdom of the Shinto religion, but Temmu died in 686, before this information was ever formally recorded.

"Records of Ancient Matters"

Although there was still no sacred book of Shinto, the religion continued to play an important role in the affairs of state. In 701 the Japanese government set up an office of Shinto affairs known as the Jingikan, or "office of *kami*." The Jingikan appointed a high-ranking official to ensure that the *kami* were properly revered throughout the land. This official oversaw the affairs of Shinto priests and monitored property where sacred shrines were built. With this formal government oversight, Shinto was assured a place in Japan's national life.

Meanwhile, the collection of information first ordered by Temmu continued, and in 708 Empress Gemmei came to power. In November 711 the empress ordered a court official named Yasumaro to write down the information that Arè had been memorizing for more than twenty-five years.

A painting of Prince Shotoku accompanied by two women. Shotoku is known as the Father of Japanese Culture for his promotion of reading and writing.

In 712, less than five months later, Yasumaro's work was complete. The final book—known as *Kojiki,* or "Records of Ancient Matters"—is filled with historical narratives, legends, short humorous stories, songs, and royal genealogies, detailing events from ancient times until the end of the reign of Empress Suiko in A.D. 628. As Sokyo Ono writes in *Shinto and the Kami Way:* "Though written in Chinese ideographs the style is ancient, pure Japanese and through it we can know something of the style of the earlier oral transmission [of the stories] from generation to generation. Consequently it is especially valued."[15]

The Twofold Way of the Gods

Even as the *Kojiki* was being written, Chinese and Buddhist influence were growing stronger every year. Like Shinto, Buddhism was regulated by the government, and all Japanese homes were required by law to have Buddhist altars. In addition, all families had to belong to a Buddhist temple. It was hardly necessary to make such membership a legal requirement: During religious ceremonies, colorful Buddhist temples, known as pagodas, were filled with melodious chanting, beautiful music, and the smell of fragrant incense. These houses of worship were extremely attractive to the average peasant.

Japan's native religion remained important, however, and simple Shinto shrines were often erected on the grounds of Buddhist temples so that worshipers could pay their respects to the *kami* before entering the pagoda.

Despite this conciliatory gesture, Shinto's popularity continued to be overshadowed by Buddhism. In 710 a new royal capital for Japan was established in the city of Nara, with buildings and street plans modeled on a typical Chinese city. And as Stuart Picken writes in *Essentials of Shinto,* "For the first time the indigenous faith [Shinto] faced the danger of being eclipsed by the immigrant cult. The Japanese *kami* did not seem to be on a par with the grandeur surrounding the Buddha and the awesome power of Chinese civilization."[16]

The power of state-run Buddhism was further consolidated during the reign of Shomu from 715 to 749. Shomu was the first Japanese emperor who was also a Buddhist priest.

Shomo's kingdom was severely threatened in 735, however, when a deadly smallpox epidemic swept through the capital. The desperate

Japan Is Named

Japan received much of its culture from China, along with its written alphabet, and the name Shinto for its indigenous religion. The country even took its name from a Chinese term, as Julia Piggott explains in Japanese Mythology:

"The years [A.D.] 593 to 621 are those given for the real acceptance of Buddhism in Japan. They were the years of the regency of Shotoku Daishi.... He was a law giver and a social reformer as well as being a devout Buddhist, and it is thought that the art of Japanese flower arrangement began during his regency when he insisted on having flowers put in front of his image of Buddha in his private shrine....

It was about this period that Japan received her name. Before it had been a loosely defined territory [known as] Izumo and Yamato; and it took the name of the latter province. But as the control of the court increased, so did interest in Buddhism, and with both came the flow of learning from the Asian mainland. The term Jih-pen in Chinese means 'source of the sun' and the Chinese gave this name to the land to their east. The words Nippon and Japan were easily derived from the original Chinese Jih-pen. Dai Nippon (Great Japan) . . . is a literal expression of the feeling the Japanese have for their country."

emperor decided to call upon gods of both Buddhism and Shinto to save his people. To enlist the help of the native religion, Shomo sent a Buddhist priest to the shrine of the Shinto sun goddess, Amaterasu, to ask for a favorable blessing. That night Shomo had a dream in which Amaterasu declared herself to also be a *bodhisattva*, a term for a Buddhist who has attained enlightenment but postpones Nirvana in order to help others to attain enlightenment. As Jack Finegan writes in *Archeology of World Religions:*

From here on it was easy to identify every native Japanese deity with some Buddha or bodhisattva and thus a theological basis was provided for a thoroughgoing [merger of the two religions]. The mixture of Shinto and Buddhism which thus arose in the eighth and ninth centuries, and prevailed for thousands of years, is called Ryobu Shinto, the Twofold Way of the Gods.[17]

The epidemic subsided and Shomo ordered the creation of a

huge bronze Buddha. The statue was still under construction fifteen years later, however, because workers were having trouble casting the massive statue. At this time the Shinto god of war, Hachiman, was invoked to bless the project. According to Picken, an oracle overseeing the project said: "I will lead the *kami* of heaven and earth and without fail see to the completion of the Great Buddha."[18]

In the following years, Shinto and Buddhism became intertwined religions within Japanese culture. Shinto *kami* were often called upon when Buddhist temples or monasteries were constructed. In turn, Buddhist prayers were often read at some of the three thousand *kami* shrines located in Japan. In addition, *kami* such as Hachiman were identified as both Shinto deities and Buddhist *bodhisattva*.

And while members of the imperial court practiced Buddhism, they continued to promote the belief that the emperors had divine origins as descendants of the Shinto sun goddess.

Shinto and Buddhism Intertwine

At the end of the eighth century, the capital of Japan moved to Heian-kyo, "the capital of peace and tranquility,"[19] later shortened to Kyoto. This era lasted until the twelfth century and was known as the Heian Period, and during this time Chinese influence waned as Japanese art and literature began to distinguish itself.

Shinto and Buddhism continued to mesh, however, under the leadership of a Buddhist priest named Kobo Daishi, who founded the Buddhist Shingon sect in the ninth century. Kobo preached that the ancient Shinto deities were really *bodhisattva* who had come to Japan disguised as *kami* in order to bless the Japanese people. As such, people could practice both Buddhism and Shintoism without conflict. In fact, the two religions had become nearly indistinguishable from each other. As Picken explains:

> Shinto had undergone dramatic change and transformation under the influence of Chinese culture. Externally, shrines became more colorful . . . painted in bright vermilion, with dancers using ancient Chinese costumes. People continued to venerate *kami* but the *kami* were identified with Buddhas.[20]

During the following centuries, Shinto and Buddhism coexisted as

Japanese culture flourished. Different sects of Buddhism, such as Pure Land, Zen, and Nichiren, appeared, each denomination blending some Shinto beliefs into its own. Japanese emperors continued to practice Buddhism and act as high Shinto priests, but they had little influence on government. Many clans competed with one another to preside over various regions of the country.

In 1192 a leader named Minamoto Yoritomo established a military government to rule Japan. Yoritomo was a devotee of the *kami* Hachiman, and because of this, a cult grew up around the worship of this Shinto god of war.

Yoritomo presided over a militaristic warrior clan and was himself a *shogun*, a word meaning "highest general." The *shogun* divided Japan into territories that were ruled by lords who used fierce warriors called *samurai* to maintain their power. This system would remain in place for more than four hundred years. Meanwhile, Shinto held its place in

A statue of Buddha in Kyoto, Japan. Japanese people have practiced both Shinto and Buddhism for centuries.

Twelfth-century shogun *Minamoto Yoritomo began the* shogunate *system of government in Japan that lasted over four centuries.*

Japanese society under the protection of the *shogun* leaders.

Christianity and Shinto

By the sixteenth century, European sailors were discovering new trade routes and visiting foreign lands such as the Americas and Africa for the first time. Japan, too, had become a destination for European traders.

In 1549 Spanish Jesuit priests brought Christianity to Japan. The missionaries spoke to the Japanese people, insisting that instead of 8 million *kami*, there was only one true God—Jesus—and that Shinto and Buddhist beliefs would have to be abandoned in order to worship him.

Some Shinto leaders welcomed the Christian missionaries, hoping they would weaken the powerful Buddhist influence on their country. While several thousand Japanese converted to

Christianity, most were unwilling to adopt the foreign religion.

The missionaries stayed in Japan. Meanwhile, in 1603 a *shogun* named Ieyasu, a member of the Tokugawa family, unified Japan under one centralized power. Ieyasu only ruled two years, but the Tokugawa would remain in power for more than two centuries.

The Tokugawa rulers moved the capital of Japan to Edo, present-day Tokyo, which was a small fishing village at that time. Threatened by the attempts by European priests to gain power over their subjects, the rulers banned Christian worship. The Tokugawa also imposed strict controls on the Shinto religion, taking over the management of temples and shrines, regulating ecclesiastical appointments, and even imposing restrictions on the physical movement of the emperor, confining him to his palace and grounds. Meanwhile, Buddhism was established as practically a state religion under the *samurai* leadership, with every family obligated to belong to a Buddhist temple.

Fear of European influence remained, however, and in the 1630s, the Tokugawa instituted a policy known as *sakoku*, or "closed country," decreeing that no Japanese person could leave the country, no

Catholic could enter the country, and all foreign trade was to be conducted in the city of Nagasaki only. This last provision allowed several hundred Dutch Protestant merchants to remain, but their activities were closely monitored. The closed-country rule would remain in effect for Japan until 1868.

Shinto During the Tokugawa

While the closed-country policy was in force, Japan was one of the most isolated nations in the world, with little outside influence, which had a positive effect on Japan and the Shinto. And under Tokugawa rule the country experienced two centuries of peace. Without the distractions of war, Japanese people turned their attention to classical Japanese history, literature, and art. This led to a revival of interest in the ancient Shinto traditions that was fully supported by the government, which promoted celebrations and increased funding to restore and maintain thousands of Shinto shrines.

At the same time, there was a rise in nationalism and devotion to the interests of Japanese culture. This new enthusiasm for all things Japanese led to hostility toward Buddhism and Chinese culture. Shinto scholars now said that the *kami* were not *bo-*

dhisattvas but that bodhisattvas were instead originally kami.

During this period several new Shinto sects were formed, some extremely anti-Buddhist in tone. The Kokugaku Shinto, or National Learning Shinto, movement was led by scholar Motoori Norinaga, who updated the ancient Kojiki to make it more intelligible to modern readers. Norinaga combined a divine belief in the Japanese government with Shinto practices and claimed, according to Picken, that kami were "the origin of government, ethics, and everything under the sun. [This] concept of . . . unity of worship and government . . . was the proper development of national life."[21]

The End of Sakoku

By the mid-nineteenth century, the world had changed drastically since Japan had first closed its doors in the 1630s. Powered by the steam engine, the Industrial Revolution was remaking the world. The United States, a

Effects of the Closed-Country Policy

In the 1630s, after the closed-country policies were instituted, Japan became one of the most isolated countries in the world. While trade continued with Korea and China, Japanese people were not allowed to leave the island nation and no Europeans were allowed to enter. In A History of Japan, R. H. P. Mason and J. G. Caiger state that this policy was a factor that allowed Japan to prepare for the modernization in a characteristically Japanese way. They write:

"Japan did not participate in the great scientific discoveries of seventeenth-century Europe and the early stages of the industrial revolution. In 1650 the country had been more or less the technological equal of Europe; two hundred years later this was demonstrably not the case. On the other hand, thanks in part to closure, Japan was free during these centuries to make significant national developments in political and social organization, and also in commerce and culture. Above all, she did not suffer the fate of many Asiatic countries . . . of having a ruling class so permeated with Western influences that it eventually became hopelessly alienated from the masses. Japan remained cohesively Japanese, and was able not only to preserve but to gain strength from her national characteristics when hit by the full tide of Westernization after 1850."

country that hadn't even existed in the seventeenth century, was now one of the wealthiest and most powerful countries in the world.

Meanwhile, the feudal *shogunate* system was beginning to collapse in Japan as Western nations such as the United States, France, and England began the process of colonizing Asia. The powerful Western countries demanded that Japan open its ports and markets to foreign traders, and in 1853 Commodore Matthew C. Perry of the U.S. Navy sailed into Edo Bay to advance this agenda.

After a year of diplomatic wrangling, the Japanese signed the first of a series of treaties that spelled the end of the closed-country policy. The Tokugawa *shogunate* was ill-equipped to deal with the new foreigners, and in 1867 its long rule came to an end.

With the fall of the *shogunate*, political power was given to Emperor Meiji, who moved the imperial palace from Kyoto to Edo. He renamed the city Tokyo, or "Eastern Capital." During the period known as the Meiji Restoration, Japan underwent

Commodore Matthew C. Perry's ships (pictured) sailed into Edo Bay to pressure Japan to open up its ports to trade.

Emperor Meiji (seated, with sword) and his family. Meiji reestablished Shinto as Japan's official religion in 1869.

an extraordinary change from an agricultural society dominated by *samurai* to an industrial powerhouse.

The pervasiveness of Shinto principles has been credited for this incredible transformation by helping people unite and work for the common good under the banner of progress. Power was restored to the emperor, who was able to unify and mobilize Japanese citizens under a central leadership, unlike the divided system of governance established under the *shogun*. And under the tutelage of the emperor, Shinto was restored to a favored place by the government.

State Shinto

With the restoration of imperial powers, Meiji wanted to reinvigorate Shinto worship and return it to its place as Japan's national religion. On April 25, 1869, a program of Kokka, or "State Shinto," was instituted. Meiji conducted a Shinto ceremony for national leaders, reciting *norito* to the *kami*. After the ceremony Meiji read the Imperial Charter Oath that made Shinto the official Japanese religion. As R. H. P. Mason and J. G. Caiger write in *A History of Japan,* State Shinto "went back to Yamato legends celebrating the divine descent of the ruling house as the linchpin of the moral and natural order."[22]

The government created a ministry to officially oversee Shinto. This department could name priests, who until that time inherited their position through their families. It could also dismiss priests who spoke or acted against official government policy.

In order to increase his power among the people, the emperor, who was also the head Shinto priest, required all citizens including schoolchildren to express their loyalty to the state and its leader through Shinto ceremonies. Children were taught absolute loyalty to the emperor as a descendant of the *kami* and unwavering patriotism to Japan as a land created by the *kami.*

Buddhism and Shinto, two religions that had been cojoined for centuries, were separated. The government ended support of Buddhist shrines across the country, and Shinto art and statues were removed from pagodas. Like *sakoku,* the old system of Ryobu—or "Twofold Way of the Gods"—was over.

Shinto in the Twentieth Century

During the first half of the twentieth century, Japan—a country that had been at peace for hundreds of years—found itself embroiled in a series of ever more destructive wars. And nationalists misused the Shinto belief that the divine sun goddess had given the Japanese power above all others to justify the country's aggressive moves in each case.

The bellicose period began when Japan attacked the Russian navy at Port Arthur, China, in 1904. Although the Russo-Japanese War lasted little more than eighteen months, the government enacted a series of nationalist policies, using the war as a justification. These changes would profoundly affect Japan for another four decades.

With the nation on a war footing, State Shinto was expanded to increase social control over Japanese citizens. The government's financial support of Shinto priests was increased, and in turn the priests enthusiastically taught patriotism and supported Japan's expansive militaristic policies.

The most substantial change during the Russo-Japanese War was the glorification of war dead at local shrines. Tens of thousands of Japanese men had been killed in the war,

A photo taken in 1904 shows half-sunken Russian ships in Port Arthur, China, during the Russo-Japanese War.

and most people had a father, son, uncle, or neighbor in the military. As such, observance of shrine rites became nearly universal throughout the country, and although it wasn't written into law, most people felt obliged to attend shrine ceremonies. In addition, the government, through local shrine administrators, kept strict watch over citizens, who were expected to support their local shrines by offering time and money. Those who belonged to small Shinto sects or other religious movements were intimidated into renouncing their beliefs, and some sect leaders were even jailed.

The Gods of War

During World War I, between 1914 and 1918, the Japanese sided with Great Britain and the United States.

Their war activities were mainly limited to further expanding their territory by seizing several German-held islands in the Pacific. By the time the war ended, Japan's economic and industrial base, along with its military powers, had made it the most powerful nation in east Asia, on an equal standing for the first time with England, France, and other European countries.

Although the war had ended, Japanese civilians did not return to peacetime life. Boys as young as fourteen continued to be drafted into the military, where they were taught to give their lives for their divine emperor.

During this era the training of Shinto priests was completely paid for by the government, and ever more money was provided both for the priesthood and shrine management. Priests were also allowed to teach in public schools with no further educational training. Many used this opportunity to further indoctrinate the young and teach all Japanese history through a Shinto filter.

In 1931 Japan seized the Chinese province of Manchuria. In 1937 the island nation invaded northern China, and by 1939 one-third of China was under Japanese rule. By this time World War II had begun in Europe, and on December 7,

1941, Japan bombed the U.S. Pacific Fleet at Pearl Harbor, Hawaii. During the next three years, Japan and the Allied forces, led by the United States, fought fierce battles over control of the Pacific.

Japanese soldiers fought with a seeming fanaticism—often against a much larger foe—that struck fear into the hearts of their enemies. They were urged on by the deeply instilled Shinto belief that their emperor was descended from the gods and dying for him would make them *kami*. Japanese pilots committed suicide by flying airplanes loaded with dynamite into U.S. ships. These men believed that they were guaranteed to become *kami* and were called *kamikazes,* or "winds of the gods."

The Overview of World Religions website details the method in which Shinto officials instilled obedience in the Japanese people under the State Shinto system:

The central role of the emperor in national and political life was symbolised . . . by frequent rituals of veneration directed to the emperor's portrait. In schools from 1890 onwards the portrait of the emperor was revered and the [doctrine] "Imperial Rescript on Education" which instilled Confucian virtues of loyalty and obedience was reverently recited. In public gatherings including those at [Shinto and] Buddhist temples and Christian churches the *kokumin girei* or "people's rite" came to be compulsory. This began as a moment's silence in honour of the war dead and by 1945 had developed into a practice of turning towards the imperial palace, singing the national anthem and reading an imperial rescript.[23]

The Shinto-based blind devotion of the soldiers could not save Japan from destruction, however. American bombing missions over Japan destroyed hundreds of factories, homes, and government buildings. And U.S. bombers deliberately targeted Shinto shrines in order to break the spiritual backbone of the Japanese war effort, damaging about 15 percent of Japan's Shinto shrines, or more than sixteen thousand buildings. And by 1945 the United States had destroyed ninety major

Six Japanese kamikaze *pilots during World War II. Pilots who flew the suicide missions believed they would become* kami.

Japanese cities, including two—Hiroshima and Nagasaki—with atom bombs.

Shinto, which had brought stability and peace to the Japanese people for centuries, had been co-opted by government leaders for purposes of conquest and destruction of others. After the war, as Japan was rebuilt from the ashes, Shinto also underwent a rebirth. Drawing on the ancient—and peaceful—roots of their native religion, the Japanese people used the strength of Shinto to sustain them through dark and tragic times. And just as the image of Japan would become overwhelmingly positive during the following decades, so, too, would the religion that had given so much to Japanese culture.

chapter | two

Lessons of the *Kami*

People who practice the Shinto religion today can trace their beliefs system back to the prehistoric age of the *kami*, when gods, goddesses, mythical heroes, and talking animals walked the earth. Legendary Shinto tales of love, jealousy, forgiveness, pettiness, conceit, selfishness, and rage are meant to provide examples about the unpredictability of human nature and the natural world from which the *kami* are born.

While most of the world's religions rely on such cautionary tales, Shinto differs from other religious beliefs in that it has no supreme deity giving moral mandates or written commandments for its people to follow. As Ono writes: "Unlike Buddhism, Christianity, and Islam, Shinto has neither a founder, such as Gautama [Buddha] the Enlightened One, Jesus the Messiah, or Mohammed the Prophet; nor does it have sacred scriptures such as the sutras of Buddhism, the Bible, or the Qur'an (Koran)."[24]

Shintoists simply believe that they personally are descended from the godlike *kami* and are expected to act accordingly in society. Shinto worshipers rely on their own inherent moral code to govern their daily lives.

The Creation of the Universe

While not considered a sacred text, the most revered book among practitioners of Shinto is the *Kojiki*, written around

A.D. 712. Basic Shinto beliefs are spelled out in the *Kojiki* and form a foundation for the religion itself. According to the *Kojiki*, in the beginning there were five Separate Heavenly Deities who sprouted forth in heaven like reed shoots in a lake. These deities created a generation of gods and goddesses, two of whom were Izanagi and Izanami, whose names translate into "He-Who-Invites" and "She-Who-Invites," respectively.

According to the *Kojiki*, Izanagi and Izanami descended from the Floating Bridge of Heaven on a rainbow and came down to an oily floating mass that resembled a jellyfish. The two had been given a Heavenly Jeweled Spear decorated with precious stones and were told by the other deities: "Complete and solidify this drifting land!"[25]

Izanagi stirred the ocean with his spear, then they both pulled it out of the water. The earth that dripped down from the end of the spear was piled up and became an island called Onogoro. The two deities set up residence on the island, created a spacious palace, and made love. Afterward, according to *The Sacred Scriptures of the Japanese:*

She-Who-Invites, speaking first, said, "O comely and lovable youth!" At that He-Who-Invites said, "O comely and lovable maiden!" When they had thus spoken, he was displeased and said, "I am the man and of right should have been the first to speak. How is it that you, on the contrary, spoke first? This is unlucky."[26]

The two deities were later married, but because of the bad luck, the child born from their union was the Hiruko, the leech-child, who still could not stand upright at the age of three. Because physical imperfection in a deity was unthinkable, Hiruko was placed in a reed boat and set adrift.

The Creation of Life and Death

After Izanami gave birth to a second deformed child, the gods ordered Izanagi to speak first after a union and the couple's luck improved. Soon Izanami produced the rest of the Japanese islands, and many *kami* who inhabit the islands, including various sea and river deities and gods of wind, trees, mountains, plains, waterfalls, and herbs.

Finally Izanami gave birth to the god of fire. This was a traumatic experience that caused her to be mortally burned. After she died, Izanami descended beneath the earth to the underworld—Yomi—the Land of Gloom.

Izanagi deeply missed his wife and traveled to Yomi to search for her. He found her and tried to bring her back to the surface, but it was very dark and Izanagi could not see his wife. Izanami begged her husband to leave without looking at her, but Izanagi lit the tooth of his comb. The flame revealed Izanami in a state of decomposition covered with maggots. Izanagi was gripped by fear and fled in panic, pursued by ugly hags of the underworld.

Izanagi barely escaped Yomi, and as he exited Izanami screamed after him that in revenge she would kill one thousand people a day. Izanagi replied that he could create fifteen hundred people a day.

Thus, according to this story, the first couple not only created human life, but ensured that people would die. As Picken writes, however, Izanagi's pledge to create life in spite of his wife's threat is "taken as [an] affirmation of the power of life over death, a strong and consistent theme in Shinto thought."[27] Indeed, Japanese culture still balances an awareness of death as a natural occurrence with the belief that physical death itself exerts a polluting effect.

The Celestial Reins of Power

After his encounter with the filthy and polluted underworld, Izanagi proceeded to a river to wash and purify himself. Izanagi cast off his clothing and jewelry, and *kami* sprang from these items. As he washed his face, three *kami* were born: Susano, the god of storms; Tsuki-yomi, the god of the moon; and Amaterasu, described by Vihar and Anderson as "nature's creator and the progenitor of the Japanese imperial line. She is the Great Divinity Illuminating Heaven, goddess of the sun."[28]

Two of the gods created by Izanagi while washing in the river went on to create day and night on earth. According to the *Kojiki*, Susano was unhappy with his job as god of the storms. He was also jealous of his sister's great power. His despair made him weep and howl, causing mountains to fall and rivers to run dry. After a bitter confrontation, Susano chased his sister, the sun goddess, into a celestial cave, causing darkness to fall across the earth. The other *kami* were greatly distressed by this darkness and used both practical and magical means, including dancing, to lure Amaterasu out of her cave with a mirrorlike silver disk.

Light returned to the world, but for his bad behavior, Susano was banished from the celestial heavens and sent to live in the lower world in the province of Izumo, Japan. Eventually, after committing several good deeds, Susano was allowed to return to the heavens, leaving behind his descendant, a benevolent *kami* named Okuninushi, the "Great Lord of the Country," who blessed the Japanese people.

Heavenly Power on Earth

Soon Amaterasu sent her grandson Honinigi to descend from the heavens and rule Japan. As symbols of his power and authority, Honinigi carried three cosmic items: a sacred mirror, a magical sword, and a string of jewels called *magatama* known for their powers of fertility.

Honinigi had to strike a deal with Susano's descendant Okuninushi to decide who would rule the world. The two powerful *kami* decided that Okuninushi would rule the invisible world while Honinigi would rule the visible world. Eventually Honinigi is said to have become the great-grandfather of Jimmu, the first human being to rule Japan. For the past twenty-six hundred years, all emperors have claimed descent from Jimmu as well as from Honinigi and Amaterasu, the sun goddess.

While these deities are central to Shinto belief, there are dozens of other important *kami,* as described by Littleton:

> Other prominent kami include [the warlike] Hachiman . . . and

Amaterasu (center), the Shinto goddess of the sun. The modern imperial family traces its lineage back to Amaterasu.

Tales of Susano

The stories of the ancient kami *attribute several legends to the deities. In* Japanese Mythology, *Julia Piggott explains the many roles of Susano:*

"Susano . . . is not entirely limited to his role as Storm god. His name has been translated as 'Swift-Impetuous-Deity' and 'The Impetuous Male.' He was banished from [heaven] and went to the province of Izumo on the coast of the Sea of Japan in Honshu. From there he was said to have planted forests on the coasts of Korea from the hairs of his beard, and because of this he is associated with forests in general. He is depicted as being heavily bearded and is perhaps connected with the hairy Ainu [the indigenous tribe of the Japanese islands; unlike modern Japanese, the Ainu were characterized by heavy facial hair]. . . .

Many other stories are told about Susano in good or evil guise. One of the most popular tells how he killed an eight-headed dragon in Izumo. He did this by making it drunk with eight bowls of *sake,* the Japanese alcoholic drink made from distilled rice. In one version the *sake* is poisoned. Susano used his courage and cunning to kill the dragon in order to rescue a minor goddess, a girl, whose many sisters had been eaten . . . by the dragon. The heroine in the story was the last surviving daughter of the family and as could be expected, she married Susano. Their children pass into the mythical history of Japan and beyond.

In the tale of the dead dragon, Susano found the sword which is another part of the imperial regalia. . . . [He] gave it to [the sun goddess] Amaterasu. In return she gave him some of her jewels, which form the third part of the regalia. On another occasion she gave him other jewels which he used as hail and lightning in his capacity of Storm god."

the "Seven Lucky Gods" *(Shichi-fukujin),* each of whom personifies a desirable characteristic or condition. The most popular of the Lucky Gods are Daikokuten, who is typically depicted with a large sack slung over his left shoulder, and Ebisu, who carries a fishing-rod in his right hand and a sea bream under his left arm. Sometimes said to be father and son, Daikokuten and Ebisu both personify wealth and material abundance. The others in this group include Benten (skill in music and the arts), Fukurokuju (popularity), Hotei (contentment and magnanimity), Jurojin (longevity) and Bishamonten (benevolent authority).[29]

Divine and Earthly

The stories of the *kami* fill many pages in the *Kojiki*, which then moves seamlessly into the actual history of Japan's early emperors. Picken comments on this concept:

> It is a strange . . . religion from a Western . . . point of view that could speak of a god dying. The gods by nature are immortal, and the idea that a man [in this case an emperor] in later ages becomes a god is also difficult to express. . . . With no seeming sense of gap, the narrative flows quite freely . . . from the timeless era of the *kami* to the historical Japan. . . . [The] narrative . . . continues to weave myth and history together even as the historical eras begin to dawn.[30]

It is this easy flow between the age of the *kami* and factual history that have given Shinto practitioners the belief

that humans include traits that are both heavenly and of the earth. The Japanese word to describe this concept is *hito*, which means "a place where the spirit is." Herbert describes this combination of the divine and the human: "[Man] is a being living under the blessing of the *Kami* . . . but he is also designated 'green-man-grass' . . . comparing the human race to green grass which

A shrine to Hachiman, the god of war, in Kamakura, Japan. Hachiman is one of the many kami *that make up the Shinto pantheon.*

grows up in a thriving manner, it clearly stresses his earthly nature."³¹

Shintoists also embrace a belief in an eternal spirit or soul. This concept in which the body dies but the vital force lives on is referred to as *tamashii*. Unlike the Western concept of the soul, which remains with a person until death, the *tamashii* may leave the body and reenter it at a later date. There are even ancient stories of two men whose *tamashii* have left their bodies at the same time and came back into the wrong bodies later on.

It is also believed that plants, animals, and other parts of the natural world have their own *tamashii*, and this living soul-like entity allows seemingly inanimate objects such as trees or rocks to possess lively *kami* spirits. With these *tamashii* representing human, animal, and natural objects, a person may seem to possess the *kami* of a river for a time, or even a fish. As Herbert writes, "The fisherman who wanted to catch a fish had to wait until the *[tamashii]* of the fish entered into him."³²

Reverence for Nature

Since the soul is often at one with the *kami* of the natural world, Shintoists possess a deep respect for nature. The power and beauty of nature is perceived as a manifestation of heavenly powers. The driving force behind phenomena such as rainstorms, volcanoes, waterfalls, and ocean waves are believed to be guided by the hands of the gods.

To channel natural energy in a positive manner requires people to seek blessings of the *kami*. And each *kami* is believed to have a divine personality that responds to sincere prayers. This idea is simply stated by B. A. Robinson in the Religious Tolerance website: "Nature is sacred; to be in contact with nature is to be close to the Gods. Natural objects are worshipped as sacred spirits."³³

Because of the oneness of the human soul with other spirits, the Japanese people believe that they are descended from heaven and are direct ancestors of the sun, in the form of the *kami* Amaterasu, the sun goddess. As Naofusa Hirai writes on the web page "Shinto: A Portrait": "In Shinto, it is common to say that humanity is 'kami's child.'"³⁴

Importance of Family and Ancestors

Since all humans are descended from *kami*, reverence for ancestors and deep respect for family is an important characteristic of Shinto. Ono expands on this idea:

Man is a child of kami, he also is inherently good. Yet there is no clear line of distinction between himself and the kami. ... [M]an owes his life, which is sacred, to the kami and to his ancestors. He is loved and protected by them. He is endowed with the life and spirit of the kami, but at the same time he receives life from his parents, grandparents, and ancestors through countless ages. Man is dependent for his continued existence on both nature and society. He is a social being. He cannot live in isolation.[35]

Because of this deep-abiding belief, Shintoists are not guided by individual wants and desires, but by the needs of the family and clan, or even the entire nation. People perceive themselves as members of interrelated families—individualism and egoism have little place in Shinto society.

The most common Shinto family unit is known as the *dozoku*, which may consist of up to thirty-five families—many branch families under the guidance of a main family. People in these entities share the same surname and are linked though patrilineal relations, meaning that they trace ancestral

descent through the male line. As Ichiro Hori writes:

The main family, or its head, possesses political, economic, and spiritual authority, and has the responsibility of overseeing the daily life of all the branch families. In turn, members of the branch families are obliged to serve the main family spiritually and materially....

The relationship between the main family and the branch families ... is reflected in mutual aid in daily life. This [cooperation] is especially apparent on such occasions as the building or thatching of a house, well sinking, and at the times of births, marriages, and deaths.[36]

Each *dozoku* has its own particular shrine at which family *kami* are worshiped. These clans also share cemeteries. And members of each *dozoku* hold annual memorial celebrations for their ancestors.

The Shinto respect for ancestors extends far beyond the *dozoku*, however. As Hirai writes: "[In] terms of our contemporary contacts with people of the world, we must revere the life and basic human rights of everyone, regardless of race, nationality, and creed, the same as our own."[37]

Ancient Shinto Beliefs

In Essentials of Shinto, *Stuart D. B. Picken examines descriptions of religious beliefs taken from Japan's oldest texts. He lists a few of the features of Shinto that were most likely in practice by the third century:*

"*Animism.* This belief sees life and divinity in all the phenomena of Nature from lightning to the winds and rain. The ancient Japanese gave these names and called them *kami.* The oldest Japanese [belief] was . . . that ancestral spirits resided in nearby mountains, coming down in spring to assist the community through harvest and returning after the fall.

Nature Worship. Closely linked to animism, nature worship is the general Japanese reverence for nature and the origin of shrines in places of great natural beauty. . . .

Ancestral Reverence. This is found in Japan as in most Asian nations. . . .

Agricultural Rites. [These] appear in references to the *kami* of the stars breaking down divisions between rice-fields. The principal shrine festivals coincide with sowing, harvesting, and the cycle of rice cultivation . . . showing how profoundly Shinto is related to the agricultural year. . . .

[Ritual Bathing]. Bathing in rivers to be rid of pollution has long been associated with Japanese culture. . . . Purification is one of the most distinctive ideas of Shinto that lies at the root of Shinto's most central and common ritual. . . . The ocean, lakes, rivers, and waterfalls are all used. It has been suggested that the Japanese fondness for the bath may be traced to the idea of [ritual bathing] as a central religious concept."

A terraced field on the Japanese island of Honshu. Many Shinto festivals correspond to the agricultural seasons.

A family looks on as a baby's name is formally registered after a Shinto naming ceremony. Family identity is a basic concept of Shinto.

Venerating the Dead

The *dozoku* family circle provides a sense of belonging that is very important to Shinto practitioners. And this family group includes family members both living and dead.

Concern for those who have passed on has been an important part of the Shinto religion since ancient times, and there are three separate categories of ancestors that are revered by believers: the recently departed, nameless ancestors who have faded from living memory, and outsiders.

The recently departed are simply members of the family who have died within the memory of those still living. Survivors of a recently departed ancestor prepare a sacred tablet listing the dead person's accomplishments and good deeds. This is preserved on a small family shrine, called a *kamidana,* or "god-shelf," reserved for the dead. It is not unusual for Shinto worshipers to gather at this altar daily to speak to the departed and to honor their memory. Littleton describes part of the daily ritual:

An elderly member of the household, often the grandmother, tends the *kamidana* by placing on it each morning small cups of saké and dishes containing a few grains of rice and vegetables . . . because all *kami* must periodically be nourished if they are to perform at peak efficiency.[38]

Special ceremonies are held each month for the dead on the day that person died. For instance, if a person died on May 12, he or she would be honored on the twelfth of every following month. More solemn services are held on yearly anniversaries, especially the first, fifth, tenth, twentieth, and so on. During these rituals, relatives gather and drink sacred sake (rice wine) and talk in detail about the commendable deeds performed by the dead. Sake is also offered to the dead. David W. Plath explains how a dead soul is honored:

> Like all members of the household [the dead person] has a right to continued affection and "human feeling" from the others. It joins all the members, living and dead, at periodic household gatherings, especially at New Year's and Midsummer. More importantly, the living help the departed soul celebrate the [anniversary] of its death-day. This may continue for upwards of 50 years . . . until no one remains among the living who knew the departed personally. At this point the departed is retired into the ranks of the nameless ancestors. Personal tablet and selfhood are destroyed.[39]

The second category of the dead mentioned by Plath are those who have faded from living memory. Their names are listed in tablets with other ancestors and kept on a family shelf, but they are revered in a more impersonal way. As Plath writes: "The soul melts into the household 'choir invisible,' an everlasting and unnumbered [multitude]."[40]

Finally, there are the outsiders— homeless souls who are not direct descendants of the family but who are affiliated in some way. These might include favored servants, housemates, friends, or others whose souls are close by but who will eventually leave to find their

Shintoists honor their ancestors with offerings of food. Here, an offering is placed on a large leaf by a gravestone.

own families. These souls are not given space on the family shelf but are sometimes given their own shelves outside of the house. Plath describes their plight: "Presumably they are quite unhappy over their situation—[that is,] having died away from home, or having no heirs to care for them—and they deserve at least an occasional charitable nod."[41]

Whatever category the dead belong to, they have specific responsibilities to their household, providing moral support and guidance for family members. For instance, Shintoists are expected to be upstanding and successful people lest they shame themselves before their ancestors. Ancestors also provide comfort for the Shinto believer, providing a basis of security no matter how far he or she travels from home.

Speaking to the *Kami*

Family shrines found within the home are also used as a place where Shintoists can speak directly to their ancestors as well as other *kami*. As Herbert writes:

It is a peculiarity of Shintô that the devotee should periodically report to the Kami what has happened to him, not apparently

for approval, or criticism, or forgiveness, but merely for information. Members of the household report every morning to the Kami on the family shrine what has happened to them during the last twenty-four hours. And children coming back from school inform their ancestors on the same shrine of the marks they have been given before they tell their own parents.[42]

In addition to reporting to the *kami*, believers also use family shrines to offer praise to the *kami* and to pray to them. Although petitioning the *kami* for personal benefits such as money, a good job, or improved health is not discouraged, it is believed to be more virtuous to pray for others. As such, people are more likely to begin their devotions by asking the *kami* to bless their community, the emperor, or even the entire nation.

People who require personal intervention from the gods might ask a family member or Shinto priest to offer prayers for them. In the case of a sick person, the priest would not ask for a divine miracle, but instead ask the *kami* to grant success to the doctors treating the petitioner.

Certain ritual movements must be performed when speaking to the *kami* before a shrine, including hand clapping, called *kashiwade*. Standing before the shrine, the devotee bows deeply from the waist and then puts the palms together in front of the face. The worshiper then claps two, four, or eight times, and bows again twice. These ritualistic movements are repeated after the prayer.

Some believe that the noise simply attracts the attention of the *kami;* others say that it is a method for the gods to take the individual worshiper by the hand. But Masahisa Goï, a Shinto scholar, gave Herbert the complicated explanation that loud hand clapping "causes 'divine' vibrations; those overcome and replace the 'human,' 'dirty' vibrations, bring down the 'white light' and heal physical and other diseases."[43]

With such importance given to hand clapping, the various vibrations are believed to contain subtle meanings and reveal the state of mind of the worshiper. Some Shintoists can predict how their day will turn out by the sound of their clapping during the morning ritual.

Evil Spirits

Not all *kami* are considered friendly and beneficial to humans. There are many evil spirits haunting the living, and these also have their place within the Shinto religion.

The Japanese word for malevolent spirits is *onryo,* meaning "spiteful or grudge-filled spirits."[44] Others are called *goryo,* or "august spirits," because they are powerful and must be treated with deep respect and placated so that they do not inflict harm upon mortals. In *Matsuri: The Festivals of Japan,* Herbert Plutschow describes the most terrifying of the *onryo:*

The type of spirit most feared by the ancient Japanese was that of a powerful person who had suffered an injustice. Elaborate *matsuri* repeated at intervals helped to placate them and to prevent harm to the entire nation. The more powerful a person had been in life, the more his unplaced spirit was feared. Consequently, the Japanese feared the spirits of emperors, imperial princes, ministers, high-ranking aristocrats, and the numerous victims of violence and war the most.... [The] degree of evil a spirit could inflict depended very much on the power or status he enjoyed. ... The malevolent spirit of someone of national importance could potentially create havoc on a

Mourners and a monk pray during a ritual to honor the dead at a shrine in Osaka, Japan.

national scale, whereas the evil spirit of a peasant could cause damage only locally.[45]

These wronged spirits not only harmed individuals who had caused their untimely demise, but were also thought to cause natural disasters such as the floods, drought, disease, fires, and earthquakes that disturbed the lives of thousands of people.

The Curse of Death

While some of these wronged spirits are believed to cause major damage, others join the ranks of the *gaki,* or "hungry ghosts," who wander the earth in an eternal search for physical nourishment and spiritual solace. These ghosts may enter the bodies of those who have just died and are feared by the living who have recently lost a loved one.

Since Shinto belief holds that the act of dying, though unavoidable, is a form of pollution, Shintoists have few traditions surrounding the recently deceased. Since ancient times cadavers were not allowed near shrines or on the grounds surrounding them. Shinto priests did not have specific funeral rites, and therefore most Japanese people adopted Buddhist traditions when caring for dead relatives. In fact, laws enacted during the Tokugawa era between 1603 and 1868 obligated Buddhist priests to oversee the burial of all dead.

Shinto priests, meanwhile, only cared for the *kami* who resided in their shrines. All rites performed by the priests were for the benefit of the *kami*, not for the relatives of the dead. Performing funerals was simply believed to be outside the priesthood's sphere of influence and not their responsibility.

Purification and Cleanliness

Since death, evil spirits, and wandering ghosts are equated with uncleanliness and physical pollution, ritual purification and physical cleanliness are very important to Shinto practitioners. And like so many other Shinto beliefs, the roots of such practices can be traced to the *Kojiki*, when the deity Izanagi washed himself in the river after his journey to the polluted underworld, where he came into contact with his decomposing wife. His bath during which the sun goddess was born gave rise to the Shinto practice of ritual bathing in streams, rivers, or the sea.

Ritualistic bathers wash away impurities, called *tsumi*, which may be interpreted to mean pollution, sickness, or disaster. There are two main types of *tsumi*, including *Ama-tsu-tsumi*, which relates to cosmic disasters such as the type Susano wreaked upon the sun goddess Amaterasu, causing her to hide in a cave and cast the world in darkness.

Kuni-tsu-tsumi are impurities caused by earthly *kami*, listed by Picken as "afflicting [with] injury or death, immodest behavior, . . . certain contagious diseases, damage done by harmful birds, wounds, . . . and other things that may be beyond human control."[46]

There are three ways to purify oneself to remove *tsumi*. The first is *harai*, purification ceremonies performed by priests, who wave purifying wands with paper streamers over individuals, groups, or objects to be cleansed. When this ceremony is held to purify the nation—or even the entire world—it is called Ōharai, or the "Great Purification."

Purifying the physical body with water is known as *misogi*. This may be done symbolically, using a small amount of water, or in a more intense way by bathing in a river, stream, or ocean. Herbert explains that there are important rituals surrounding *misogi*:

The Spirit after Death

Although corpses are considered unclean by Shintoists, the spirits of the dead are believed to live forever in various worlds beyond this one. This concept is explained by the Shinto priests (for whom English is a second language) who write for the Shinto Online Network Association website:

"According to the Shinto faith, a human spirit is believed to remain forever like the spirit of Kami does. . . . The most well known other world is 'the other world of Heaven' where the most venerable deities live, and then it comes to 'the other world of Yomi' where [the] divine female parent who gave birth to the land of Japan live[s]. This world is long considered to be underground, and it is believed to have the connection with the habit of burial of the dead. . . . The third other world is called 'Tokoyo' which is believed to exist somewhere beyond the sea. According to the folk faith . . . there is a belief of 'the other world in the mountains.' This faith has the connection with [the] fact that grave yards were on a hill which has a panoramic view over a village and also a fact that people often expressed their wish to watch their descendants even after their death. These other worlds, however, are not described [as] a utopia nor as a hell. There is no difference at all from this world. It reflects a faith in the spirit of the dead who can visit this world if people make a ritual to revere the spirit. . . . It can be said that Shinto is not a religion which centralized its interests in the life after death, but in this world."

Wooden and stone markers commemorate the dead in a Shinto cemetery in Tokyo. Shintoists believe that the spirits of the dead live on forever.

[In] order to reap the full benefit of his *misogi,* the Shintoist should follow some definite rules during the period immediately preceding. [Generally] speaking, he should take simple food in small quantities and follow a vegetarian diet, abstain from alcohol, tea and coffee, take a cold bath or a cold shower after his daily hot bath, change his underclothing every day and spend more than one hour in meditation both morning and evening....

When bathing in cold water for *misogi* purposes, it is said that water should first be splashed over various parts of the body in the following order: the mouth, the face, the private parts, the chest and abdomen, the feet and legs, the shoulders and arms, the back, the chest and abdomen again, and finally the whole body. To be complete, the cold bathing . . . should take place successively at the mouth of a river, near the source of a river, in the sea, under a waterfall and in a spring or well. The last mentioned exercise provides one of the reasons why most large [Shinto shrines] have a small artificial lake in the precincts.[47]

The final method of purification is *imi,* or "avoidance," in which a person avoids certain words, phrases, or actions. For instance, the word *kiru,* or "cut," is considered bad luck to use during a wedding. A more drastic example of *imi* is when the mother or father of a high priest dies. He is thought to be polluted for one year following the death and must eat with different utensils than other family members, while living in a special room built near the house. In the past this period of isolation would be imposed for three years, but it has been shortened in recent times.

Salt Purification

Salt plays a very important role as a purifying agent in Shinto ceremonies. The white crystals are believed to thwart evil, and salt is used in many places in daily life in Japan. Mourners at funerals receive small, elegantly wrapped packages of salt to sprinkle on their doorsteps when they return home. This is done to keep the pollution of death from entering their dwelling. Bars, restaurants, and other places of business keep two small piles of salt outside their doorways, and entryways are washed with salt water in order to attract customers.

Salt is also used in sumo wrestling, a popular Japanese sport that has its roots in ancient Shinto tradition. Sumo matches have taken place in Japan for at least two thousand years and were originally held as amusements for the *kami*. Today auditoriums where the bouts are held may seat up to ten thousand spectators.

Every facet of the sumo match is governed by ancient Shinto tradition. The canopy over the wrestling ring represents the roof of a shrine. Shinto priests perform ritualistic ceremonies at the beginning of each sumo match, and the ring is blessed with Shinto prayers. Before entering into a match, each sumo wrestler takes a symbolic bath, washing his mouth and hands. As in prayer before a shrine, wrestlers clap their hands to send out vibrations to the *kami*. They also stamp their feet to drive away evil spirits. Before entering the ring, each man tosses a handful of salt into the air to purify the area. Like many other aspects of modern Japan, sumo has primeval tradition at its very core.

The Magic Way

Shinto is an incredibly complex religion with innumerable legends surrounding the deeds and actions

Shinto men participate in a misogi, *or ritual bath, to purify themselves as part of their New Year's celebration.*

A sumo grand champion (right) performs a ring-entering ritual at the Meiji Shrine in Tokyo.

of the *kami*. Each deity has its own devotees, with countless traditions, shrines, celebrations, and prayers dedicated to these children of the celestial heavens. While Shintoists live in the busy modern world, many take great comfort and pride in the ancient roots of their religion. As a guiding force for millions, the lessons of the *kami* are not forgotten by a nation grateful for their supernatural powers.

chapter | three

Shrines and Priests

Those who practice the Shinto religion often pay respects to the *kami* deities several times a day. This may happen at small family altars within a home, at simple outdoor sanctuaries, or at elaborate Shinto shrines found all over Japan.

Devotees visit shrines for any number of reasons, as Littleton writes: "A mother may visit a shrine to petition the local god to help her child pass a difficult university entrance examination, or an elderly gentleman might ask the same kami to find his granddaughter a suitable husband."[48]

Since Shintoists believe that the entire nation is touched by *kami* and that the spirits reside everywhere, shrines, or *jinja*, are found in most villages, towns, and cities in Japan. Large metropolitan areas such as Kyoto and Tokyo have dozens of shrines.

Each shrine has its own guardian *kami*, but some deities may have several shrines built in their honor in cities and towns throughout Japan. And while most shrines are made for only one *kami*, many have smaller shrines located nearby for lesser spirits.

Wherever shrines are located—from busy cities to the rural, out-of-the-way forests—the entire surrounding community is responsible for the upkeep of the building and grounds.

In addition to *kami* worship, these grounds, called precincts, may also be used as a place for picnics and community events, much like parks. The area around the shrines is considered sacred, however, and kept spotlessly clean and well tended despite sometimes heavy use. Shrubs, trees, flowers, and other foliage are planted to inspire devotees. As Ono writes:

[Once] a kami has been enshrined, the precincts, like the shrine itself [*sic*], acquire a special sanctity; and every effort is made, when the surroundings themselves are not naturally beautiful or impressive, to create a beauty which will instill in the minds of the worshipers a mystic sense of closeness to the unseen divine world and to nature. The natural beauty imparts to the worshiper a religious impetus to move from the mundane to the higher and deeper divine world, which can transform his life into one of closer fellowship with the kami.[49]

A Home for the *Kami*

Although there are more than eighty-one thousand shrines in modern Japan, Shintoists of ancient times had no formal buildings to house the *kami*. Instead, the devout gathered in places of great natural or unusual beauty, such as lightning-struck trees, strangely shaped volcanic rocks, rushing waterfalls, towering mountains, or other areas. These celestial spots were said to be *yorishiro*, or "the place of the *kami*." These areas were often marked only by ropes made from rice straw.

Ancient shrines near stands of trees were called *himorogi*, which roughly translates to "all living trees" or "sacred trees." Those near interesting or unusual rocks were called *iwasaka* which were also believed to house the *kami*. And it was in these places that Shinto rites were performed by worshipers.

Around the sixth century A.D., Shintoists began to construct small *jinja shaden*, or shrine buildings, that resembled their grain-storage buildings or homes. This shrine-building program was inspired by the Buddhists, who were building pagodas of majestic beauty throughout the country. Shintoists also wanted attractive shrines to remind the Japanese people of their native religion. The religious significance of the buildings is explained by Herbert:

Formerly the Kami resided exclusively in the Plain of High

Heaven ... and when the devotees wanted them to come down, they asked them to descend into the *himorogi*, where they were welcomed. ... [At] the end of the ceremony, they were dismissed [to return to the heavens]. ... Now the temple [permanently] houses ... an earthly manifestation of the Kami and he no longer has to be asked to come [down from heaven].[50]

Shinto worshipers do not choose the specific locations of shrines. Instead, they ask the *kami* to choose the site and relate their choice to devotees through dreams, divination, meditation, or other mystical means. For instance, if a clan felt that it needed protection from a specific rice *kami*, clan members might ask a local shaman to communicate with the spirit and ask it where it would like to reside.

Since *kami* are nature spirits, shrine locations are most often determined by the natural environment. For instance, the Hiryu Shrine, or Shrine of the Flying Waterfall *Kami*, is located at the Nachi Waterfall, which descends from a great height and produces a

A torii *stands in the water at the shrine on Miyajima Island. Shrines were traditionally located in places of exceptional natural beauty.*

purifying mist that envelops the surrounding area. This spot seems obvious as the most auspicious site for such a shrine. Other shrines might be located at special rocks, the confluence of two rivers, near ancient trees, or by other natural features. Some shrines are situated in such rural wilderness that only local residents know of their location.

In large cities, however, shrines might be found in tiny parks, on the rooftops of high-rise apartment buildings, and on busy streets near automobile traffic, pedestrians, restaurants, and bars. As Ono writes:

> All too often in downtown metropolitan areas shrines have been forced by circumstances beyond their control to give up the original beauty of their surroundings and be satisfied with an almost barren site totally devoid of foliage. This is ordinarily the result of population pressures which have transformed a relatively secluded site into a throbbing commercial or industrial center. In some cases, of course, the location is due merely to the availability of the site, and without any meaningful ties either to land or to the city.[51]

Shrine Buildings

Kami decide upon not only each shrine's location, but its architectural features as well, and each deity has a specific style of building. For example, a shrine with a twin-peaked roof built to house Hachiman, the god of war, looks different, from a shrine with a triangulated, mountainlike roof that accommodates Yamasuie, the *kami* of Mount Hie.

Ancient Shinto shrines were constructed from bamboo and thatch, which were prone to decay. Around the seventh century A.D., shrine builders sought to make longer-lasting shrines, utilizing unpainted, rough-hewn wood, stone, and other materials that lasted for centuries. In fact, Japan boasts several shrines built in the eleventh century that are some of the oldest intact wooden buildings in the world.

The basic design of Shinto shrines was firmly established by the eighth century. The oldest structures look like ancient granaries—single-room dwellings with peaked roofs built on raised platforms.

More sophisticated shrines were constructed to look like the multistoried homes of nobility. Deeply revered as sacred spaces, these shrines were built utilizing

The Grand Shrine at Ise

Of all of the eighty-one thousand shrines in Japan, the most important is Ise-jingu, located on the main island of Honshu, southeast of Tokyo. C. Scott Littleton describes the shrines in Eastern Wisdom:

"The most sacred of all Shinto shrine complexes, the Grand Shrines at Ise ... are dedicated to two major divinities: the rice goddess, enshrined in the 'Outer Shrine' *(Geku)*, and the sun goddess, Amaterasu, celebrated in the 'Inner Shrine' *(Naiku)*. The latter holds the sacred mirror, one of the prime symbols of the sun goddess, which was supposedly brought to earth by Amaterasu's grandson, Honinigi.... The emperor [of Japan] traditionally makes an annual pilgrimage to the *Naiku* to report the year's events to his divine ancestor as well as to pray for a good year's rice crop.

The [shrine at] Ise is distinguished from other Shinto shrines by the fact that it is torn down and rebuilt every twenty years (the most recent rebuilding occurred in 1993). This custom, which began in the 8th century [A.D.], serves by extension to renew the enshrined divinities. The new shrine buildings, which are located on carefully maintained sites immediately adjacent to the previous ones, are identical to the ones they replace; the carpenters responsible for the rebuilding typically come from families who have participated in this activity for generations. Thus, the Ise shrines are steeped in ancient tradition, but at the same time always appear new and fresh."

considerable time and talent. The various designs feature verandas, sweeping roof lines, several entrances, and elaborately carved ornamentation. Not all shrines project such ageless splendor, however. Newer shrines located in busy cities may be simply built from concrete and steel, which are favored in some areas because,

unlike wood and thatch construction, they are resistant to fire.

No matter where the shrine is built, before its construction an ancient ritual known as *Jichinsai* is performed so that people may show their respect for the local *kami* and pray for good luck and absence of misfortune during the building's construction.

A Sacred Dwelling Place

Just as shrines have changed over the years, so, too, has Shinto. The oldest form of the religion practiced in the most ancient manner is called Folk Shinto. The belief system associated with the emperor is called Imperial Household Shinto. But with tens of thousands of shrines located throughout Japan, Jinja Shinto, or Shrine Shinto, is the most popular form of the religion today. And as Picken writes:

To completely describe Shrine Shinto as it exists in modern Japan would require a detailed history of every shrine, its buildings, and *kami*, clearly a task beyond the scope of one book. It would in fact become a [81,000-] volume series! So diverse is the variety of rituals and ideas that generalizations invariably break down.[52]

Despite the many different practices and customs, there are many

The Heian Jingu shrine in Kyoto. The interior of a shrine is accessible only to the priests and kami, *while practitioners worship outside the building.*

similarities between the various *jinja*. For example, shrines are constructed exclusively for *kami* spirits, while devotees gather outside the building to worship. The only humans to ever enter the buildings are priests, who perform rituals within. The interiors are simple but aesthetically pleasing to the senses. Even in the busiest cities, the shrines remain quiet sanctuaries where worshipers will not be distracted in their quest to experience the presence of *kami*.

Each shrine has several sacred objects that make the site holy or are used by priests during rituals. The most important object in a shrine is the *shintai*, or the "divine embodiment" of the *kami* who lives there. This is kept in a silk-lined box in the sanctuary, or *honden*, behind two swinging doors that close off the shrine's innermost chamber. The object is kept behind a bamboo curtain, and not even the priest can see it.

The shape of the *shintai* and the material it is made from are closely guarded secrets, and often the high priests themselves do not know what the object is. As Herbert writes:

It is generally enveloped in a number of precious cloths, cas-

kets, etc. to which more are added as the previous ones show signs of wear, and no one may—or will—commit the sacrilege of opening the many protective layers. It is believed, however, that in a great majority of shrines the object . . . is a mirror.[53]

The *shintai* may also be a natural object such as a rock, tree branch, or even the remains of an animal. For example, since the tortoise is the guardian *kami* of one Japanese fishing village, the shell of a tortoise is used as a *shintai* in a local shrine. Other seaside villages use precious stones that have washed ashore over the course of the centuries.

Other Shrine Artifacts

The *shintai* is the only representation of the *kami* in the shrine—there are no pictures, paintings, or statues of the spirit. There are, however, several other important objects within the shrine dedicated to the *kami*. One of the most significant is the mirror, always present even if not used as a *shintai*. The mirror represents the silver disk mentioned in the *Kojiki* that was used to lure the sun goddess Amaterasu out of a cave after she was chased there by Susano the storm god.

Later in the story, Amaterasu sent her grandson down from heaven to rule Japan with a sacred mirror, a magical sword, and a string of jewels. Ono quotes a fourteenth-century text that talks about the significance of the mirror:

> The mirror hides nothing. It shines without a selfish mind. Everything good and bad, right and wrong, is reflected without fail. The mirror is the source of honesty because it has the virtue of responding according to the shape of objects. It points out the fairness and impartiality of the divine will.[54]

In addition to the mirror, banners painted with heavenly symbols such as the sun, moon, sky, and clouds represent the presence of the *kami* within the shrine. A string of jewels and a sword along with a halberd and shield are hung from the posts that hold the banners. These items represent, according to Ono, "the power to defend the *kami* from evil and the power of the *kami* to protect justice and peace. . . . [T]he mirror, jewel, and sword . . . symbolize the virtues of wisdom, benevolence, and courage respectively."[55]

Other sacred objects include the *gohei,* or "symbolic offering." This upright wand with strips of angled white paper also signifies that the *kami* is present within the sanctuary.

A hallowed object similar in appearance to the *gohei* is the *hari-gushi,* or "purification wand," with long paper streamers. This is used by the priest, who waves it over worshipers or objects when performing the *harai,* or "purification rites."

Sacred rice straw ropes, known as *shimenawa,* are also used within shrines or on the grounds to show that this is a sacred place where the *kami* choose to dwell. Each cord may be as small as a piece of string or as thick as a rope six feet in diameter. Pieces of zigzag-cut rope or cloth, called *shide,* hang from the *shimenawa* to represent offerings to the *kami.*

The Graceful Gateway

The entrance of each shrine features a gateway, known as a *torii,* which marks the border between the finite world and the infinite world of the *kami.* The *torii* consists of two upright posts made from wood, rock, metal, or even concrete. Some *torii* have beautifully designed cross beams on top, while the traditional ancient structures have a *shimenawa* strung between the uprights. Other more elaborate *torii,* such as those with three sides or peaked upper

Paper of the Spirits

The ancient art of folding paper was brought to Japan from China around the sixth century A.D. Called *ori-kami*, or "origami," the word translates as "paper of the spirits."

Origami had ancient spiritual uses in the Shinto religion long before Japanese writing was developed. People folded the paper into various objects, whispered prayers over them, and tied them to trees. It was believed that when the wind blew over the origami figures, the prayers would be amplified. Out of respect for the tree *kami* that gave life to the paper, the origami figure was never cut with a knife or sharp object, only folded.

The custom of bringing origami to Shinto shrines is as old as the art form itself and continues today. One of the most popular origami figures is that of the crane, which is a symbol for peace and good luck. Thousands of origami cranes are left as offerings at Shinto shrines every year.

beams, are occasionally built at the entry to shrine grounds.

Torii may also be found at natural shrines in rural regions, standing before the rock, tree, or waterfall that is considered sacred. In some cities, such as Kyoto, one or more *torii* stand above public sidewalks and roadways, where they remind passersby of the presence of *kami* even in the busy city.

After passing beneath the *torii*, devotees often feel an upwelling of spirit, but they must be purified because, as Ono writes, "no one with any illness, open wound, flowing blood, or in mourning should worship at shrines."[56]

There are four objectives of a devotee at a Shinto precinct, according to Herbert: "reporting, thanking, praising, and praying."[57] It is here that people tell the *kami* of the special events in their lives, thank them for their blessings, praise them for their goodness, and pray for continued happiness, health, and wealth for their families.

The Shrine Pathway

After passing under the *torii*, visitors walk along a path, called a *sando*, often made of pebbles, dirt, or sand. This reminds visitors of the natural, peaceful environment of the shrine grounds. The path is often laid out at a crooked angle because Shintoists are not supposed to turn their backs on the *kami* when leaving.

Devotees approach an ablution pavilion—a stone trough filled with water. After removing their coats, hats, and scarves, worshipers use a long-handled bamboo dipper to take a symbolic *misogi*, a purifying bath. They lightly rinse their mouths and splash water on their hands. This ritual allows them to stand unpolluted in the presence of the *kami*.

The torii, *or gateway, represents the border between the finite world and infinite world of the* kami.

On approaching the shrine, guests pass by statues that serve to protect the shrine and ward off evil spirits. Influenced by Buddhist statues, these are usually lions or dogs. These statues are believed to be benevolent in character but possess fierce humanlike faces to drive away negativity and evil. Picken describes them:

> There are several variations. Sometimes both have horns, sometimes neither has. Sometimes both are open-mouthed or closed-mouthed. Most frequently, one mouth is open and one shut. They are usually made of stone but in some cases of bronze or wood. Their role is . . . to prevent bad spirits from entering the shrine precincts.[58]

Statues that represent *kami* are also occasionally used outside the shrine as guardians. Some resemble ancient warriors with swords in their belts and arrows on their backs. Others represent an animal, such as a fox, monkey, horse, or deer, that the guardian *kami* is thought to embody. Occasionally local people who have achieved some sort of honor or fame—such as a famous sumo wrestler—may also be represented by statues.

A worshiper at an ablution pavilion uses a bamboo dipper to take a misogi. *Shintoists splash water on their mouths and hands before entering a shrine.*

Other objects along the shrine path include lanterns made of stone or bronze and memorial tablets that describe important local historical events. The lanterns are usually donated by community members, business associations, or companies.

The devotee finally arrives at the place for prayer known as the *haiden*, or "oratory." Ono describes the experience:

In front of the worship hall, after placing his hat, scarf, and overcoat to one side, the worshipper may jangle a bell, if there is one hanging over the offering box. This drives off evil spirits and produces a calm feeling by its pure sound. Then he stands quietly and performs the simple acts of devotion by tossing a coin (in rural areas sometimes a few grains of rice wrapped in paper) into the offering box . . . offering a silent prayer and bowing twice deeply, clapping the hands twice at the level of the chest, bowing once deeply and then only slightly before turning away. (Sometimes a written prayer is read, but this is rather rare.)

If the occasion is one of special significance and the shrine facilities are adequate, the worshipper may make his wishes known at the shrine office and, after presenting a small [amount of] money or material gift, he and those with him are taken into the oratory or sanctuary. There, sitting on the mats behind the priest who faces the inner sanctuary, a more formal ritual is observed, which includes the reading of a prayer, indicating among other things the date, occasion, names of the participants, and the presentation of a sprig of *sakaki* [sacred Japanese evergreen] as a token offering. Before the ceremony begins the money or material mentioned above is placed by one of the

shrine staff on the offering tables.[59]

After worship is over, devotees might walk around the precinct and browse at the commercial stalls staffed by young women called "altar girls," who sell good-luck charms, amulets, postcards, and things people can take home for use on their personal altars. These items are not sold outright but exchanged for monetary donations.

Shinto Priests

Most major precincts are managed by local associations that hire priests to manage the shrine and grounds. In large cities such as Tokyo, shrines might employ up to thirty priests. In smaller districts, shrines pay priests to visit their

Shinto priests prepare offerings for a ritual in Kyoto. Large shrines may have as many as thirty priests.

precinct to perform rituals and cere-monies. Large or small, all shrines must have priests in attendance to perform important rituals. Ono describes the priesthood and its function:

> Being primarily a ritualist, a priest must know how to con-duct the rites, ceremonies, and festivals, including the prepara-tion and intoning of the appro-priate [prayers]. This training can be secured either from other priests [or] by attending classes. ... Such training qualifies a per-son without further examina-tion for one of the four grades of the priesthood. ...
>
> Each shrine is in charge of a chief priest *(gûji)* but a large shrine may have an assistant chief priest *(gon-gûji)* and sever-al other priests of the two lower ranks *(negi* and *gon-negi).* At Ise Shrine, there is also a High Priestess *(saishu).* This is an ancient office which tradition-ally has been held by an Imperial princess.[60]

In ancient times there was no for-mal priesthood, but rather groups of individuals, called shamans, who were believed to possess magical powers. These people, many of them women, were well-respected within their communities for their abilities to communicate with the *kami.*

As clans grew larger and more powerful, male family leaders became head priests and performed the most important ceremonies while choosing other, lesser mem-bers of the community to effect minor rituals. As the government grew in size and the imperial court took on more importance, priests who oversaw Shinto rites for the emperor and entire nation were ele-vated to the level of nobility. By the eighth century A.D., the priesthood was officially elevated to the Office of Divine Affairs, which held a very important role in government, out-ranking even the emperor's top advisory board.

The Priesthood Today

Since World War II, priests have had no official government status but continue to attract great respect from the Japanese people. They are appointed by the Association of Shinto Shrines, an organization that oversees all of Japan's shrines. Some follow their fathers into the priesthood, and several families have been serving in the priesthood for centuries, although the hereditary system was formally abolished after the war. Some important shrines, however, are served only by those with a long family background in the priesthood.

Others who wish to join the priesthood can do so by attending schools where they can learn to recite traditional *norito* and liturgies and learn Shinto ritual. This may be done at the Faculty of Shinto Studies at Kokugakuin University in Tokyo or at Kogakkan University in Ise.

There are six grades to which a Shinto priest may aspire: the Superior, the First, the Second, the Semi-Second, the Third, and the Fourth grades. There are also four ranks within this system: the lowest is the *chokkai,* or "uprightness"; next is *seikai* or "righteousness"; then *meikai,* or "brightness." These ranks are based on a person's education, training, and shrine experience. Those above these ranks are called *jokai,* or "purity"—priests who have at least twenty years of experience.

Although the job has traditionally been held by males, during World War II women began serving as priests while their husbands were fighting the war. Oftentimes the men did not return and the women remained in charge of the shrine.

After the war the Association of Shinto Shrines allowed women to serve as priests, and today there are about two thousand female priests of about twenty thousand total.

Today priests live with their wives and families often in homes built on shrine precincts. While there are some who serve as full-time priests, many clerics have other jobs and only serve the shrine on a part-time basis. In rural areas not served by professional priests, festivals and rites may be performed by community members who hold the job on an annual rotating basis.

Daughters of priests also play an important role in Shinto worship. Young single women, known as *miko,* dress in white kimonos and perform ceremonial dances called *Kaguramai,* or "sacred dance for the kami." After they have been married, however, *miko* can no longer perform these dances.

A Day at the Shrine

The day begins as early as 6:00 A.M. for priests performing their recurring rituals. The head priest in his traditional costume opens the doors of the worship hall and recites traditional prayers, or *norito,* to the *shintai* representing the *kami* within. When this is done, food offerings are left on a nearby altar.

Priestly Garb

Jean Herbert describes the clothing worn by Shinto priests in Shinto: At the Fountainhead of Japan:

"The priestly robes . . . in Shintô temples are characterized by that unostentatious refined beauty which permeates all forms of Japanese art. . . .

One of the most typical items, which forms part of most if not all ecclesiastical dresses, is the *hakama*, a wide split skirt which falls down to the ankles. It may be of various colours: white, light blue and, for the high dignitaries, of purple silk. With the crest of the temple woven in the material it is with a few exceptions . . . reserved to the [high priests] of the temple.

The upper part of the dress is generally composed of two or more layers of what Westerners call kimono, with very wide and very long sleeves, occasionally almost trailing to the ground. According to their actual shape, colour and usage, they are called by various names. . . .

Over them come other garments, of more or less the same shape, which also bear a variety of names: the *hô*, which may be black, red or light blue and which may be worn over any of the above; the *kari-ginu*, an informal outer robe, which may be of a dozen different colours according to the age of the wearer and the season of the year. . . .

There is a considerable diversity of headgear, varying according to the rank held by the priest, but apparently still more according to the type of ceremony and the part which he plays in them. When not actually officiating, he is practically always bare-headed.

The simplest type is the black *eboshi*, which may be worn with the . . . *kari-ginu*. . . . The *kaza-ore*, which is somewhat more sophisticated, is made of the same black stiff wide-meshed lacquered silk."

These priests both wear the hakama, *an ankle-length split skirt, and a kimono with wide sleeves.*

Junior priests then prepare the shrine for the public, sweeping or raking the gravel or dirt on the *sando* and washing the stone statues that line the path. At 8:00 A.M. the priests and staff gather in the shrine offices and recite another *norito*. The gates are then opened to worshipers.

The public business of the shrine is described by Picken:

A shrine is a place of activity every day, all year round. Weekends tend to be busier because people have leisure time to take their cars for road safety purification or to seek *oharai* [purification] for personal reasons. People who do so go to the shrine office and register and then wait for their turn to have the rituals performed. They pay for these services, which enables the shrines to receive an income. Parishioners may also make appointments for priests to perform rituals at their new homes or their companies or to mark a special event in the family. Even casual visitors may be eligible for such services if the shrine kami is well known for some special capacity, such as assisting at childbirth or in passing examinations. In such ways, shrines offer care for all aspects and stages of life.[61]

Sometime between sunset and 9:00 P.M., after a full day of public visitation, the food offerings are removed from the inner altar and the shrine is closed for the evening.

Back to Nature

While people communicate wishes and prayers to the *kami* at crowded shrines every day, Shinto remains a religion closely associated with the contemplative glory of nature. No matter how awe inspiring a busy shrine precinct may be, the buildings and grounds are still the work of humans, not gods. And as Ono writes: "No amount of artificial beauty is an adequate substitute for the beauty of nature."[62] So while a shrine in a busy city might play an important role in daily Shinto worship, Japanese people—who are renowned for their love of travel—try to make pilgrimages to shrines located in wilderness areas at least once a year.

The Japanese islands contain hundreds of soaring mountains, and the *kami* are said to dwell at the summits of several of these mountaintops, called *reizan,* or "spirit mountains." Some spirit mountains are considered so sacred that only

More than 100,000 pilgrims climb Mount Fuji each year. Pictured here are devotees at Koya, one of the many temples on the summit.

priests are allowed to climb them. There may be a *torii* at the top, or an oratory, but rarely a formal shrine.

The most famous spirit mountain is Mount Fuji, the dwelling place of the *kami* who is honored as the great-grandfather of Jimmu Tenno, Japan's first emperor. An active volcano towering nearly 12,400 feet above Tokyo, Mount Fuji is known throughout the world as a symbol of Japan. Over 100,000 devoted Shintoists make the grueling pilgrimage to the top of Mount Fuji every year. This is an eight-hour climb made in special straw sandals that can only be attempted in July and August when the mountaintop snow has melted. Many pilgrims try to climb all night so they can see the sunrise from the summit. At the edge of the volcanic crater at the summit, there are several shrines where devotees can worship.

At the other end of the spectrum, there are several caves in Japan where *kami* are said to dwell. One of the most famous places to visit the *kami* underground is the Udo Shrine, where the spirit of Jimmu Tenno's father is said to have been born.

Just as mountains and caves are sacred places of the *kami*, so, too, are some islands. The Itsukushima Shrine near Hiroshima, for instance, is where Shintoists worship the *kami* that is the island Miyajima.

While the grandiose mountains and deep caves are some of the most stunning examples of *kami*, Shintoists may worship something as simple as a tree or a grove. From rooftop shrines on concrete apartment buildings to elaborate temples visited by millions, Shinto devotees understand that the *kami* are everywhere and venerate them in places from the ocean shore to the soaring volcanic peaks of Japanese legend.

chapter | four

Ceremonies and Celebrations

Shinto is a religion rich in ceremonies and celebrations both personal and public. The timing of each celebration is based on the ancient agricultural calendar that follows the circle of seasons throughout the year. Shinto devotees perform ceremonies before spring planting to ask the *kami* to bless their rice crops. As the grains grow, rites are held to petition the gods for help in keeping away harmful pests and natural disasters. Festivals of thanks take place during the harvest, and New Year's celebrations are held to purify and renew worshipers for the coming year.

In addition, with the strong Shinto focus on ancestors and community, countless rituals are held to honor guardian *kami* of clans and pay respects to deceased family members.

While some ceremonies are solemn, many are astoundingly colorful and happy affairs with elaborately decorated costumes, joyous dancing, and widespread merriment. And while these look like secular celebrations, they are serious religious festivals that involve worship, reverence, and prayer.

Family Rituals

The most personal Shinto ceremonies revolve around life's important passages, such as marriage, childbirth, and coming-of-age.

As in many cultures, Japanese marriages are a time for family gatherings and celebration. In centuries past, Japanese marriages were traditionally arranged between two families rather than by the bride and groom. And until the nineteenth century, weddings were simple celebrations held in the home. Since that time, however, arranged marriages have gone out of style, and it has become more common for ceremonies to be held at reception halls on shrine precincts. It is during this time that couples ask the *kami* for protection and blessings for themselves and the children they hope to have.

Traditionally, weddings were performed after the harvest season, and October remains the most popular month for Japanese weddings. Couples today might be married in modern Western-style clothing—bridal gowns for the women and tuxedos for the men. Traditional Shinto wedding attire, however, may still be seen on occasion.

A traditional Shinto bride wears a beautiful silk kimono and a tall wig with a white headband that is said to "hide the horns of [female] jealousy."[63] The groom also wears a finely made kimono and divided pants. The traditional ceremony is described by Herbert:

A priest makes offerings to the Kami to the sound of sacred music. A *miko* [ceremonial dancer], with ritual gestures, serves sake, first to the bridegroom and then to the bride, twice; they drink it according to

A bride and groom stand before the miko *while the groom drinks the sacred sake.*

a special rite, *san-san-kudo*, the name of which is sometimes given to the whole ceremony. After which both offer [a sacred tree branch] to the Kami. The time then comes for the intervention of an elderly couple, husband and wife, who play more or less the part of god-parents; the lady, who has been standing behind the bride, puts on her finger a ring which a *miko* has brought in a jewel-case. After that, the god-parents and one guest from each side of those present offer [the sacred tree branch]. Tables are then set for the newly-wed couple on one side at the back of the room, and for the god-parents on the other, also for guests alongside the two side-walls, and a small meal . . . is served.[64]

Birth of a Child

Japanese people place a high value on family, and children hold an especially esteemed place within the family structure. When a woman becomes pregnant, there are several Shinto ceremonies that take place, the first one beginning before the baby is born.

By the fifth month of pregnancy, it is believed that the soul has entered the fetus and that the unborn child is under the protection of the *kami*. At this time a simple ceremony is performed in which an eight-foot-long strip of white silk—part of the wedding headdress—is temporarily wrapped around a pregnant mother's body for protection.

After a baby is born, there are several ceremonies performed that are meant to ensure health and happiness. The first is the naming ceremony, where the baby is introduced to family and friends and given a name often chosen by a godparent. The mother does not attend this ritual because she is believed to still be unclean from childbirth.

The next rite takes place when a close relative transports the baby to the local shrine on the thirty-second day after birth for boys and the thirty-third day for girls. This is the first time the newborn is taken out of the home, since it is believed that the child's soul is not stable for about one month. At the *miyamairi* ceremony, the child is made an official parishioner and the family renews its commitment to the local shrine while establishing a relationship between the child and the *kami*. Later a feast is held. Again, the mother is not allowed to attend this rite.

On the 120th day of life is the "eating for the first time" ceremony,

A Shinto priest holds a purification wand over a baby's head to ward off evil during a naming ceremony.

during which the child is given its first small bits of solid food. This is the first ceremony attended by the mother since the baby's birth.

As the child grows, other rituals are held. On November 15, when boys are three and five years old, and girls are three and seven, chil-dren visit their local shrines dressed in traditional clothing. After being blessed by the priest, the children ask the *kami* for protection and pray for approval from society. On their ninth birthday, children attend a ritual in which their long hair is cut into styles worn by adults.

Girls' Day

While Shinto families practice many ceremonies involving children, Japan is famous for huge annual public festivals enjoyed by the entire nation.

March 3 brings Hinamatsuri, or the "Doll Festival," which is also called Girls' Day. Following the ancient agricultural calendar, this festival arrives in early spring when fragrant peach blossoms adorn the

Family Ceremonies

Many Shinto ceremonies are family affairs with several branch families gathering with the main family of the clan. In Religion in the Japanese Experience, *Ichiro Hori gives the details of the Bon family's schedule of celebrations in the first and seventh months of the year.*

"Thirteenth to sixteenth of the seventh month.—This is the time . . . the Bon branch family goes to the main family to help make rice cakes *(mochi)*, the most important and sacred food of the New Year and other festival days and ceremonies in Japan. . . .

First day of the first month.—The men of the branch families usually visit the main family to give greetings on the New Year; the host and hostess of the main family give them special food and sake in return. . . .

Fifteenth of the first month.—[There] is a mock celebration of rice planting in the garden of the main family's house. . . .

Thirteenth to sixteenth of the seventh month.—This is the time of the Bon [family] festival (memorial services for the spirits of ancestors and all souls of the dead). Members of branch families clean the ancestors' tombs (usually stone monuments) in the main family's graveyard on the thirteenth day. Early in the morning of the fourteenth day, members [of the families gather] in order to celebrate the Bon festival; they clean the house and prepare the ornaments and new altars for the coming spirits or souls from the other world. After this, all members of the [family] group go to the graveyard with offerings and worship at their ancestors' tombs. . . . On the afternoon of the sixteenth day . . . [families gather] to honor the ancestors' spirits as well as all the souls enshrined in the special altars and to say good-bye to those who are returning to the other world."

trees in Japan. It is a season of planting and ritual purification to exorcise the symbolic uncleanliness of winter.

During this time, families with young female children gather to pray for their health and happiness. They eat red, white, and green lozenge-shaped rice cakes called *hishi-moch,* and even small children are allowed to drink the sweet white rice wine called *shiro-zake.*

Expensive dolls called *hina-ningyou* are central to the festivities. Made specially for the holiday, the doll sets consist of fifteen figures: the lord and lady, three ladies-in-waiting, five musicians, three guards, and two retainers. In modern times, some of these traditional dolls have been replaced by famous Japanese cultural heroes such as actresses, singers, and sports figures. The dolls sit on exquisitely made miniature furniture surrounded by eating utensils, musical instruments, mirrors, and other items. During a ceremony, they are given symbolic offerings of tricolored rice cakes, sake, and peach blossoms.

Many doll sets used on Girls' Day are worth thousands of dollars and are handed down from mother to daughter with new furniture and objects added each year. Babies experiencing their first Girls' Day

are likely to receive special dolls from their grandmothers at this time.

Another festival, involving paper dolls, takes place on March 3. This celebration, known as Hinamatsuri, is based on the ancient Shinto tradition of rubbing paper dolls over a person's body to wash away impurities and evil spirits. These dolls—also considered *kami*—are then floated down a river, which takes the bad influences with them to the sea. In some rural regions of Japan, the Hinamatsuri ritual is particularly popular, and hundreds of paper dolls may be seen floating in rivers during this time.

The Boys' Festival
Dolls also play an important role on the May 5 festival Tango no Sekku, or "Boys' Festival." On this national holiday, Shinto shrines and private homes fly colorful carp-shaped streamers outdoors while displaying warrior dolls indoors.

Like Girls' Day, Tango no Sekku began as an ancient festival meant to drive away evil spirits. While Girls' Day uses peach blossoms that are prolific in March, the Boys' Festival utilizes May's iris flowers, whose strong odors are believed to wash away evil and purify one who includes them in a bath.

The Dolls of Girls' Day

The website Hinamatsuri—March Girls' Festival lists the details of several popular Shinto festivals providing the names of some of the dolls used during Girls' Day and the role each figure plays.

"Obina—An ancient Emperor. Paired with Mebina and wears a traditional costume....

Mebina—An ancient Empress. Paired with Obina and wears a traditional costume....

Sannin-kanjo—Three court ladies waiting on the couple above....

Taiko—A boy who plays a drum.

Fue—A boy who plays the flute.

Utai—A boy who sings or chants.

Zuishin—Two Ministers [who] attend the celebration.

Udaijin—The Minister of the Right.

Sadaijin—The Minister of the Left. Since the Left was considered superior in the old Japanese court, often an elder man known of his wisdom was chosen for this position."

Irises are linked to the warriors' motif by a linguistic accident. The Japanese word for "iris," *shoubu,* is spelled the same as the word for "battle." The flower and the festival have become linked together in rites that at one time prayed for victory and good luck among feudal *samurai* warriors.

The carp streamers—which are flown from flagpoles, balconies, and rooftops—symbolize strength and determination because carp often swim against a river's current. This is linked with a Chinese legend that states that a carp that moves upstream will turn into a dragon if it can swim up a waterfall. This legend is taken as a metaphor for a way to achieve a successful life.

Food offerings on the Boys' Festival include rice dumplings wrapped in bamboo leaves, which are also believed to keep away evil, and rice cakes wrapped in leaves of oak, a sacred Shinto tree.

Boys and girls both rejoice at a national festival called Coming-of-Age held on January 15 for people who have reached their twentieth birthday that year. Although this is a nonreligious festival celebrated by institutions such as government or business offices, many people visit shrines on this day to receive blessings from the *kami*. After this milestone in their lives, men and women may marry without first asking their parents for permission.

Matsuri

While Boys' Festivals and Girls' Days are family-based celebrations, there are hundreds of other public Shinto festivals held in Japan throughout the year. These festivities are called *matsuri*, a word derived from *matsuru*, meaning "to worship."

Matsuri first and foremost are shrine-based festivals, and most of Japan's eighty-one thousand shrines hold celebrations dedicated to their individual *kami* each year. Some festivals in large cities attract up to 250,000 exuberant celebrants, while those in small towns may draw only a few dozen people. Vihar and

Young men bow to receive a prayer by a Shinto priest at a shrine in Tokyo as they celebrate Coming-of-Age Day.

Meaning of *Matsuri*

The website Basic Terms of Shinto defines the word matsuri *as follows:*

"Worship, festival. An occasion for offering prayers, thanksgiving, reports, and praise to a deity or deities. A *matsuri* 'festival' generally starts with solemn rituals, which are followed by joyous community celebrations. The rituals center around the presentation of *shinsen* or food offerings, the recitation of *norito* [poetic words addressed to a deity], music, and worship, and are followed by a communion feast called *naorai*. The joyous community celebrations may include a procession with the deity, dancing, dramatic performances, *sumo* wrestling, and feasting. *Matsuri* are closely related to the cycle of agricultural seasons. Farmers begin cultivation in the early spring by praying for plentiful crops, and in autumn they offer thanksgiving for a plentiful harvest and present the fruits of the harvest to the gods. The word *matsurigoto* is an ancient word used to refer both to government and worship, reflecting the attitude that humans should follow the will of the gods in political life."

Devotees in a paddy field in Nara, Japan, perform the rice planting festival, one of the many matsuri *with agricultural themes.*

Anderson describe *matsuri* and their importance:

> They are, perhaps, the ultimate celebrations. Amid a spectacular display of costume, color, and age-old ritual, participants summon the gods down to earth to mingle and rejoice with them. A most eloquent form of worship, Japanese festivals are intimate, joyous encounters with the divine. Japan may well enjoy more festivals than any other country in the world. On almost any day of the year, at least one festival is sure to be under way somewhere on the archipelago, and on certain days, the whole nation seems to be in the thick of celebration. Varying in size and grandeur, some *matsuri* may involve no more than a single part-time priest and the handful of residents of a tiny farming village modestly celebrating spring planting; others may engage a cast of more than a thousand to thrill tens of thousands of onlookers with their pageantry. They encompass celebrations both rural and urban, traditional and modern, solemn and fun.[65]

To a casual observer, the sight of thousands of people in elaborate multihued costumes dancing, singing, playing music, and drinking sake on a city street may look like a parade. But these Shinto celebrations have deep spiritual meaning and provide a way for people to offer thanks, prayers, gifts, and praise to the *kami*.

Invocation, Communion, and Joyous Chaos

Large or small, each *matsuri* follows a similar three-part series of events, according to Picken, "the invocation of the *kami*, the offerings to the *kami*, and the final communion with the *kami*."[66]

The first part, the invocation, is performed by priests in ceremonial dress after they have taken the *misogi*, a ritual bath. During this time the priests recite *norito*, traditional poetic prayers, inviting the *kami* to visit with the public and join in the festivities.

Next the *shintai*, or the "divine embodiment" of the *kami*, is removed from the innermost sanctum of the shrine by important laypersons of the community. This item is placed on a portable shrine called a *mikoshi*. The richly ornamented *mikoshi* is supported between two long poles and carried on the shoulders of elaborately costumed celebrants. During this phase of the ritual, the deity is believed to be awakened from its peaceful condition to an alert, vibrant state.

After the *mikoshi* is transported from the shrine precinct, it is welcomed by the public who make offerings, or *shinsen*, to the *kami* within. People believe that by giving up the highest quality foods they can afford, the *kami* will return the favor and bless them with the best the gods have to offer. As such, offerings of beautifully prepared fish, fruit, grains, rice, rice cakes, sake, salt, vegetables, and other staple foods are piled near the shrine. After the priest makes a short speech to welcome the people to the *matsuri*, gifts such as flowers and money are also offered to the *kami*.

With the formalities finished, the most colorful part of the *matsuri* begins. Although the portable shrine contains the sacred *shintai*, it is now turned over to the teeming crowds, who dance, lurch, and stag-

Tokyo residents shout as they carry the sacred mikoshi *through a* torii *to a shrine during a summer festival. The noise and jostling is believed to please the* kami.

ger with it throughout the nearby streets. Vihar and Anderson describe this process:

> The parading of the *mikoshi*, the elaborate and weighty portable shrine and momentary home of the honored deity, is frequently the festival highlight. With the *mikoshi* borne through the neighborhood on the striving shoulders of a multitude of somewhat intoxicated celebrants, this is no solemn procession. The unrestrained, nearly ecstatic, drum-beating, chanting, cheering, and jostling are thought to be pleasing to the gods. Sharing the burden of this tremendous weight is considered a privilege by the bearers, and the feat is cathartic, effecting physical and spiritual renewal of both bearers and their enthusiastic observers.[67]

The ritualistic creation of disorder surrounding the *mikoshi* can sometimes become quite violent. People might beat on the shrine with sticks and rock it violently while pushing and shoving each other. These actions are believed to represent the sometimes unruly and energetic nature of the *kami*. The boisterous behavior of the crowd

was described in the late 1950s by renowned travel author Fosco Maraini:

> People were shouting, singing, quarreling; bare shoulders, bare chests, bare buttocks, ecstatic faces, intoxicated faces, faces in pain, faces of fawns and satyrs, seethed and swirled like a sea in torment beneath showers of sparks that vanished in acrid smoke floating away into the black tree-tops.[68]

The portable shrines are accompanied by very large, beautifully decorated floats known as *Dashi*. These are described by the Shinto priests who write for the Shinto Online Network Association:

> [Tours] of Dashi ... are prepared by groups of the community members. These Dashi are quite large. Some of them have two or three [stories], which are taller than an ordinary house. They are gorgeously decorated by fine brocade and curtains. ... In the evening, the center of a community is brightly lit by lanterns [that] hang at the eaves of each house, and on [the] Dashi [where] musicians and dancers make their performances. At

this moment, the festivity reaches its climax. . . . Since Dashi is carried by many people, they shout [in rhythmic] time and the crowd also [responds] with the encouraging shout. The festivity [becomes a frenzy, and] quarrels and some wounds . . . result. At this time, people are in an extraordinary stage. [The] common ideas [of] everyday life [are] discarded there. Emotion pent up in a daily life [explodes forth]. Energy preserved through a year is [expelled]. In a sense, busting up emotion and spending up all the energy ensure peace in the ordinary life which comes after the festival. At each household a festival banquet is prepared and thus a day of a festivity becomes the most joyful day of the community.[69]

Music, Dancing, and Theater

The musicians who ride on the Dashi play various-sized drums and rhythm makers such as tambourines and wood blocks in addition to flutes and bamboo wind instruments. This ritualistic music drives the often turbulent action during the *matsuri* and begins even before the *kami* is taken from the innermost sanctum of the shrine. It is believed that the rhythm of the instruments imposes order on celestial chaos and creates a harmonic space where *kami* can commune with humans.

The music accompanies ecstatic dancing that is also believed to attract and please the *kami*. The dancers find their tradition in the ancient story in the *Kojiki*, in which the heavenly deities performed a joyous dance to lure Amaterasu, the sun goddess, out of the cave where she was hiding from the storm god Susano.

In addition to music and dance, many annual celebrations incorporate a wide array of entertainment depending on the festival's location and historic background. Song and poetry are held in high esteem at the *matsuri* and are also used to communicate with the *kami*. The Japanese poetry form of haiku, with three unrhymed lines of five, seven, and five syllables, respectively, are believed to include the cosmic powers of the *kami*. When used in song, these lines, or "word soul," are said to call the gods to earth to create harmony between people and nature.

Acrobatic displays such as walking on fire, tightrope walking, making objects magically disappear, or even stabbing oneself with a knife

Music is thought to bring order and harmony, allowing people to be one with the kami. *Here, a man plays a flute while others clash cymbals at a festival.*

without being injured are also believed to please the *kami.* These are seen as a way for people to demonstrate their godlike nature by transcending earthly limitations such as gravity and even their own pain.

Theatrical plays are also an integral part of the festival, because the festivals themselves are actually played out like stage dramas. Plutschow explains this concept:

Many *matsuri* include theatrical plays. Like dance, people looked upon plays as a divine manifes-

tation, the way in which deities communicate with the community. . . . In its very nature and structure, matsuri is a play, an interaction of man and deity outside the real world. It takes place in a world of illusion [and merges] the present with the past in a scenario transcending reality. . . .

On a cosmic level, too, *matsuri* is a drama, bringing together people and gods. The festival allows them to interact in dramatic action and allows people to influence or dominate forces beyond their control. But, in order to affect this, the people must become that which they would dominate, representing both deities and the natural forces the deities are believed to control. When the festival deity appears, it incarnates these dangerous yet divine forces. As a drama . . . people try to influence forces beyond human control by giving them a human face and personality and forcing them to behave according to human desire and interest.[70]

Kyoto's Gion Matsuri

Such dramas might re-create historical events or mythical stories from the *Kojiki* on grand proportions. The Gion Matsuri in Kyoto, two hundred miles west of Tokyo, is one such festival based on an actual

The Gion Matsuri (pictured) originated in 869 when a priest led a parade through Kyoto to appease the kami *and stop a plague.*

event. The Gion Matsuri is dedicated to appeasing evil spirits who were believed to be responsible for a terrible plague that ravaged that city in 869. To stop the plague, a priest from the Gion shrine led a grand parade through Kyoto, hoping to soothe the angry *kami*. The deadly disease soon subsided, and since that time the event has been re-created every year, growing in scope and complexity to become one of Japan's most popular annual celebrations.

Beginning on July 1 and lasting an entire month, the Gion Matsuri features street fairs, games, and traditional festival foods such as balls of fried octopus and grilled ears of corn coated with soy sauce. The event features singing, dancing, drinking, and laughing meant to neutralize the evil nature of the plague *kami*.

The event culminates with a parade featuring thirty large, elegantly constructed floats, some of them weighing over twenty thousand pounds. Each float is elaborately decorated with a treasure trove of antiques, statues, art, intricate miniature historical scenes, and 500-year-old Dutch and Turkish tapestries. The floats carry dozens of musicians and are pulled by hundreds of men, women, and children wearing magnificent costumes. Hundreds of thousands of tourists crowd the streets to watch the procession, some wearing light summer kimonos and tall wooden shoes.

The Gion Matsuri is only one of hundreds of Shinto festivals dedicated to appeasing malevolent spirits. These celebrations have roots in ancient history when people did not understand the real causes of plagues, crop failures, and natural disasters. Yet the tradition of pacifying harmful deities continues in scores of *matsuri* held throughout Japan.

New Beginnings at New Year's

In addition to *matsuri* held for local *kami*, each shrine celebrates national annual festivals with equal enthusiasm. New Year's, or Oshogatsu, is by far the largest national and religious holiday in Japan, with celebrations lasting from December 28 until January 6. A family-based event, New Year's festivities involve several major activities with roots in the Shinto religion.

Because each year is seen as wholly separate from the last—not connected—late December is used to complete all duties and tasks. As New Year's Eve draws near, people hold *bonenkai*, or "year forgetting

The Thousand Man Procession

In 1617 the renowned shogun *Tokugawa Ieyasu was laid to rest at the Toshogu Shrine in the small mountain town of Nikko. Twice a year the people of Nikko re-create a martial spectacle known as the Thousand Man Procession to honor the* shogun. *This event is described by Gorazd Vihar and Charlotte Anderson in* Matsuri: World of Japanese Festivals:

"The resplendent Toshogu Shrine is the final resting place of the Edo era shogun and unifier of Japan, Tokugawa Ieyasu. In 1617 his remains were brought to Nikko in a grand procession befitting his rank. There he was enshrined, deified, and worshiped as a kami, as is customary in Japan for exceedingly great personages. Every year in the months of May and October when spring and autumn are in their glory, this Thousand Man Procession (Sennin Gyoretsu) is reenacted.

Offerings are placed on the altar, sacred Shinto dances are performed, and a spirited and skillful exhibition of ancient-style equestrian archery . . . is given, all seeking to please and entertain the deities. The procession begins with parish dignitaries on horseback leading companies of samurai soldiers and guardsmen, fitted out in authentic military manner of that bygone time: armored, helmeted, and bearing spears, halberds, bows and arrows, or matchlock guns. There are falconers and flag-bearers, masked lions, monkeys and fairies, with Shinto priests, sacred shrine maidens, pages, and traditional musicians adding to the numbers. Last of all come three *mikoshi*, the portable shrines which house the deities, including the sacred spirit of Ieyasu, for the duration of the festival. Crowded up and down the avenue are many thousands of spectators who, for a short time, feel their nation's illustrious history come to life."

parties," at which time people try to put their worries, bad luck, and troubles behind them.

The New Year's holiday is also a joyous event as people decorate their towns with colorful banners and festoon doorways with pine and plum branches in bamboo baskets.

People clean their homes before New Year's Eve with a ritual sweeping, or *osoji*, meant to scrub away bad luck and make room for a fresh start. Once the *osoji* is finished, rice straw ropes similar to those found at shrines are strung around the house to keep away evil and show that the space is now considered sacred.

On New Year's Eve, people engage in a traditional feast called Toshi-koshi soba, which translates to "Across the Years Noodles." At this time, thick buckwheat soba noodles are served in homes and shrines immediately before midnight so that celebrants are eating as the new year begins. At midnight shrines ring their gongs 108 times, each ring meant to eliminate a specific type of evil behavior according to the Buddhist tradition.

New Year's Day is another day for traditional meals with certain foods such as shrimp, seaweed, eggs, chestnut, and pork eaten to bring good luck in the coming year. On this day children receive money from their parents and other relatives.

Sometime between New Year's Eve and the first week of the year, the entire family will visit a Shinto shrine. This act, called *hatsu mode*, or "first shrine visit," is undertaken

Priests at Tokyo's Meiji Shrine make their way to a year-end rite in preparation for New Year's, the most important of Shinto festivals.

by more than 100 million people across the country. Picken writes of the problems this causes in one Tokyo shrine: "The *Meiji Jingii* [shrine] in Tokyo usually has 2.5 to 3 million visitors within the first seventy-two hours of the New Year. Police with microphones appeal to people to make their prayers short and keep moving to let others in."[71]

During these visits, people throw away their good-luck charms from the previous year hoping to release old evils. New charms are obtained and people make wishes upon them for the coming year.

Seasonal Festivals

Other popular celebrations include Setsubun, or "seasonal division," on February 3, the traditional beginning of spring in Japan. This celebration had been practiced since the eighth century, and in years past evil spirits were chased away by burning foul-smelling dried sardine heads and beating on drums. While this custom has fallen out of favor, some people continue to hang dried fish heads over their doorways so malevolent spirits do not enter. In addition, cooked beans, which are believed to keep away evil, are thrown inside the home to protect the family from bad luck. Later, family members

pick up and eat one bean for every year they've been alive, plus one. This ritual is said to guarantee that the celebrant will survive at least one more year. People also throw beans in Shinto shrines during the Setsubun celebration.

The website Annual Ceremonies at the Kasama Inari Jinja describes the Setsubun rituals at that shrine:

> At Kasama Inari, following completion of the official ritual at the Hall of Worship, a specially constructed platform in the shrine precincts is the site for the performance of an ancient ritual of driving out evil *(tsuinashiki)* using peachwood bows, reed arrows, and peachwood staves. Some 300 officiants dressed in traditional formal attire throw out goodluck beans ... specially prepared according to secret techniques passed down through the family of the shrine's chief priest.[72]

The bean throwers toss cash to those attending the ritual as well, and special gold emblems are distributed as charms for personal safety.

The Bon Festival

With its major focus on ancestor worship, the Bon Festival—or "Ancestral Soul Day," held for a period of three days in mid-August—is another religious holiday important to Shinto worshipers. Although it is related to the Chinese Buddhist festival Urabon Sutra, it is also part of the Shinto calendar. The reasons for this are explained on the Shinto Online Network Association web page "Folk Shinto: The Yearly Round of Observances":

[People] visit grave yards in order to recall the souls of ancestors [who] had been once sent to the [Buddhist heaven known as the] Pure Land . . . [and] all the members of a family or a clan get together to enjoy the specially prepared meal for the occasion. From these points, Bon Festivals [are] considered to be one form of the amalgamated folk faith [that have] been customarily performed in Japan for a long time.[73]

During the Bon Festival, Shintoists believe that their departed ancestors return to earth for three days to visit their still-living families. And special rituals are performed to

Women perform a dance at the Bon Festival. According to Shinto belief, ancestors come back to earth during the festival to visit their families.

liberate souls who might be trapped in hell. These ceremonies are also held with a rite called Segaki-E, or "Feeding the Hungry Spirits." At this time special altars, called "spirit shelves," are built in homes, and food offerings such as cucumber, eggplant, and rice are offered as well as flowers, incense, and purified water.

Ritual fire also plays a part in the Bon Festival, featuring paper lanterns containing candles that represent *mukaebi*, or "welcoming fires." These are placed in front of residences in order to usher ancestors into the home. *Okuribi*, or "leaving fires," are set behind homes to light the way back to the other world.

At the end of the Bon, paper lanterns are sailed down rivers or set adrift in oceans in order to send ancestors back to the celestial beyond.

Ritual, Symbol, Costume, and Color

Other popular Shinto celebrations in Japan are held in accordance with the agricultural cycle. The Haru Matsuri, or "Spring Festival," and the Natsu Matsuri, or "Autumn Festival," are of great importance to Shinto worshipers. In spring, prayers are offered to the *kami* in hopes of a good harvest. This is also a time to

hold rites commemorating the ancestors of the imperial family. In the autumn, thanks are given for the abundance of the season. At the Grand Shrine at Ise, the deities are offered the first fruits of the harvest by the emperor.

Together there are four categories of Shinto festivals, according to the Shinto Online Network Association web page "Procedures of a Worshipping Rite":

Taisai (the grand festival), Chusai (the medium scale festival), Shosai (the small scale festival) and Zassai (other miscellaneous festivals). The Grand Festivals include the annual festival to revere the enshrined deity, Spring Festival to pray for good harvest, Shinto Thanksgiving to appreciate the harvest and to share the first harvest with Kami. The medium scale festivals include a ceremony to celebrate . . . Japan's Foundation Day and New Year's Day, the small scale festivals include all the rest of [the] festivals. . . . The scale of these festivals differ from each other according to the nature of each festival.[74]

In addition to these major celebrations, there is a full calendar of

Buddhist holidays that are also popular throughout Japan. Vihar and Anderson summarize the Shinto love of celebration:

[Festivals] are the happiest and most optimistic of occasions, when personal cares are momentarily forgotten. Customarily extremely reserved, the Japanese people then appear at their sociable best, emboldened by joy, the strength of numbers, and perhaps by some sanctified sake, too. Festival visitors, including foreigners, are unquestionably welcome, and their sincere interest in the proceedings often generates a quiet pride among the celebrants. These are not secret rites for believers or initiates only, but celebrations for all who care to partake.

An indivisible part of Japanese life, festivals evolve with the times, embodying the concerns of the people. Constant throughout the thousands of festivals is the ardent appeal for good luck, health, and prosperity. In the past when life was difficult for most, well-being seemed wholly at the mercy of the kami, yet even today, the protection and sense of security they offer maintain their appeal.[75]

In the colorful, high-energy celebrations called *matsuri*, the Japanese express their desire to bind the present to the past, the secular to the religious. These festivals have long played a significant part in the spiritual and cultural life of the Japanese people and have acted as a solid basis for national unity for thousands of years.

chapter | five

Shinto in the Modern World

Japan today remains one of the world's industrial power-houses. After the near total destruction of World War II, the country was able to rebuild and reinvented itself to become one of the most prosperous and advanced countries in the world. At the beginning of the twenty-first century, Shinto holds an esteemed place in Japanese society. But it was many decades after the disaster of World War II before the religion regained broad popular support.

During the war years, State Shinto, which had been growing in strength since the 1880s, was as powerful as it ever had been in Japanese history. Social and political pressures required every citizen to attend shrine ceremonies. Emperor Hirohito was referred to as *arahitogami*, the Japanese word meaning *"kami* in human form." Schoolchildren were taught by Shinto priests that the Japanese were a master race destined to rule the world. And during the war, veneration of men who had died in combat reached an all-time high. By 1943 over 1.2 million Japanese soldiers were enshrined as *kami* at the Yasukuni Shrine in Tokyo.

When the war effort ended in a stunning defeat for Japan in 1945, millions of people became disillusioned with State Shinto beliefs. Their beautiful and ancient land—a country that had never in its history been defeated by an outside force—lay in ruins. Many people blamed the catastrophe on government propaganda that had been integrated into ancient Shinto teachings.

The Shinto Directive

The vanquished Japanese were forced to live under a new ruler—the Allied occupational forces run by United States general Douglas MacArthur, whose administration moved in to take over the daily affairs of the government. Like millions of Japanese people, the Allied forces viewed State Shinto as one of the major causes of Japanese nationalism and aggression.

Within weeks the Allied occupational forces stripped Shinto of its state support. Shrines and priests were deprived of government funding, and it was no longer mandatory for Japanese people to participate in shrine rites. These orders, combined with partial blame for the war, caused Shinto to lose its esteemed standing among the general population.

The new status of Shinto was formalized four months after the Japanese surrender. On December 15, 1945, the Shinto Directive, written by a U.S. Army lieutenant, was issued by the occupation offices that administered religious affairs. It read, in part:

In order to lift from the Japanese people the burden of compulsory financial support of an ideology which has contributed to their war guilt, defeat, suffering, privation, and present deplorable condition, and

In order to prevent a recurrence of the perversion of Shinto theory and beliefs into militaristic and ultranationalistic propaganda designed to delude the Japanese people and lead them into wars of aggression, and

In order to assist the Japanese people in a rededication of their national life to building a new Japan based upon ideals of perpetual peace and democracy,

It is hereby dictated that:

a. The sponsorship, support, perpetuation, control and dissemination of Shinto, by the Japanese ... governments, or by public officials, subordinates, and employees acting in their official capacity are prohibited and will cease immediately.

b. All financial support from public funds and all official affiliation with Shinto and Shinto shrines are prohibited and will cease immediately....[76]

The Shinto Directive

In 1945 the Allied occupational forces, led by the United States, issued the Shinto Directive, prohibiting support of the Shinto religion by the imperial ruler or the Japanese government. Quoted by Helen Hardacre in Shinto and the State, 1868–1988, *it read, in part:*

"The purpose of this directive is to separate religion from the state, to prevent misuse of religion for political ends, and to put all religions, faiths, and creeds upon exactly the same basis, entitled to precisely the same opportunities and protection. It forbids affiliation with the government and the propagation and dissemination of militaristic and ultranationalistic ideology not only to Shinto, but to the followers of all religions, faiths, sects, creeds, or philosophies. . . .

Militaristic and ultranationalistic ideology, as used in this directive, embraces those teachings, beliefs, and theories which advocate or justify a mission on the part of Japan to extend its rule over other nations and peoples by reason of:

(1) The doctrine that the Emperor of Japan is superior to the heads of other states because of ancestry, descent, or special origin.

(2) The doctrine that the people of Japan are superior to the people of other lands because of ancestry, descent, or special origin."

The directive also prohibited, among other things, financial support from public funds to pay for Shinto shrines and banned the propagation of militaristic and nationalistic ideologies in Shinto practices, rites, and ceremonies. The educational system was ordered to purge any mention of Shinto from textbooks, and student field trips to shrines were banned. In addition, portraits on altars of Emperor Hirohito were to be removed.

Separating Shinto and State

The Shinto Directive sought to clarify the difference between State Shinto, which was banned, and Sectarian and Shrine Shinto, which were still permitted. Sectarian Shinto, composed of thirteen sects founded by individuals in the nineteenth century, was protected as any other religion, and Shrine Shinto was to be allowed after all traces of state oversight had been removed.

The public, more interested in whether or not the emperor would be tried as a war criminal, did not consider how the directive would impact Shrine Shinto. And Shinto priests were simply relieved that the shrines would not be destroyed or closed.

Hirohito was allowed to retain his throne under the condition that he formally, publicly disavow the belief in his divine nature and order people to stop worshiping him as a *kami.* The emperor did so in a

Under the Shinto Directive, Emperor Hirohito was forced to discredit the belief that he was divine.

speech broadcast on the radio on New Year's Day 1946, a day when millions of Japanese people visited Shinto shrines. Hirohito also offered a guarantee of complete religious freedom to every Japanese citizen.

In 1947 Hirohito's words were adapted into law under Japan's new Constitution. Modeled on the United States Constitution, the document renounced war forever, limited the powers of the emperor, gave women the right to vote, and guaranteed freedom of religion. Article 20 states:

> No religious organization shall receive any privileges from the State, nor exercise any political authority.
>
> No person shall be compelled to take part in any religious act, celebration, rite or practice.
>
> [And the] State and its organs shall refrain from religious education or any other religious activity.[77]

Since that time these provisions have been enforced by Japanese government officials, and any appearance of state or political support of Shinto has been strictly banned.

Leaving Rural Shrines Behind

After the war, Shinto was affected by more than government decree. The demographic makeup of the country was radically changed as millions of people moved from the poverty-stricken countryside to take jobs in burgeoning big cities. These uprooted people also lost contact with their local shrines, the lands where their ancestors once lived, and even their rural families. The agricultural rhythm of planting and harvesting had little importance to people working up to sixty hours a week in offices and factories. These changes, along with the removal of state funding, dealt Shinto a severe setback.

Shinto leaders were alarmed when they lost monetary and public support. In order to prevent total collapse of the ancient native religion, they banded together to form the Jinja Honcho, or Association of Shinto Shrines, to oversee the eighty-one thousand shrines and precincts scattered throughout the island nation. They issued a statement to clarify their purpose, According to their website, it read:

The objectives of Jinja Honcho are: 1) to control and to guide the member shrines in terms of administration, 2) to preserve traditional Shinto rituals and festivals, as well as promoting the traditional morals, 3) to pray for prosperous development of Japanese society, 4) and finally, but not least, to contribute in establishing the everlasting world peace.[78]

Under the tutelage of Jinja Honcho, Shrine Shinto was rescued. Shrines, which had been largely neglected since the end of the war, were cleaned up and reopened to the public. The war-shocked Japanese people, many of whom were experiencing poverty and hardships unknown for generations in their country, were desperate for the reassuring blessings of the *kami* to help them through these difficult times.

During the six years of Allied occupation, the support of the general populace was crucial to the survival of Shrine Shinto, and the financial donations of sympathetic worshipers prevented the complete collapse of Japan's ancient system of shrines. By the time the Allies left Japan in 1952, most shrines had become self-supporting. And student field trips to shrines were once again permitted, allowing children to learn about their native religion.

Shinto Controversies

Despite the efforts of the Association of Shinto Shrines, the religion continued to face difficulties in the 1960s and 1970s. For instance, the issue of Shinto-state separation was never fully clarified by the Shinto Directive and continued to raise emotional questions for decades. One of the most controversial questions concerns the place of the emperor and the imperial household in modern Japanese society.

In the years after the surrender, there was heated debate about the degree of the emperor's responsibility for the war. Many called for an

Shinto priests at a shrine in Nikko, Japan, about 1947. Shrines suffered from the lack of government funding after the end of World War II.

abolition of the monarchy; the Japanese constitution retained the emperor but called for a greatly reduced role in which he would have no political powers and would act only as a figurehead for ceremonial functions.

This did not settle the emotional issue, and a vocal minority continued to call for an end to the hereditary monarchy, saying that such a position was counter to democratic values and that an emperor might once again lead to a rise in harmful nationalism. The majority who supported the monarchy, however, did so as long as the wall between Shinto and the state remained in place.

This conflict made headlines in January 1989 when Emperor Hirohito died. The burial of the emperor, who had led Japan through World War II, brought old wounds to the surface. Picken explains:

> When Emperor Hirohito died . . . the question of religion and state came up again. Who should pay for the funeral? What kind of funeral should take place? . . . [The] late Emperor was interred at the site of the Imperial Mausoleum [but controversy] centered on

the erection of a white *torii*, the gate to a shrine in front of the pavilion where the rites were conducted according to the Shinto tradition. The argument was whether the Imperial Household . . . should use Shinto rituals as their own personal right, or whether the national funeral should be free of religious ritual. In fact, the appearance was confusing and although the *torii* was removed, controversy ensued.[79]

Another area affected by the issue of Shinto-state separation was at the Yasukuni Shrine first dedicated to Japan's war dead in 1869. Those who died for their government are enshrined as *kami*, and the shrine acts as a monument for the war dead, but state support of the shrine, banned by the Shinto Directive of 1945, is still prohibited. Thus members of the Japanese military who died in combat in World War II are prevented by law from receiving official recognition at the shrine for their supreme dedication to the country, a restriction that has been particularly painful for their families and fellow veterans alike.

Although dozens of bills calling for state support of the shrine have

The procession at Emperor Hirohito's funeral in Tokyo in 1989. Hirohito's funeral was complicated by the fact that religion and state were supposed to be separate.

been introduced since the war ended, elected officials remain reluctant to give any authorized government sanction to the religious site.

The problem of Shinto-state separation also surrounds shrine festivals, which once depended on funding from city governments. In order to survive without official support, the festivals had to promote the *matsuri* as tourist attractions rather than religious celebrations. With busloads of tourists brought in from across the country, the once-local character of the festivals was often diluted.

Move Away from Tradition

The debate over Shinto-state separation was only one part of the religion's declining popularity in the decades after the war. As tens of millions of people moved from rural to urban areas, they left behind the majority of Shinto shrines that are located in the countryside far from the bright lights of the big cities. Although hundreds of urban shrines have been constructed, many of the new sites were never as popular as those located in traditional natural settings.

This problem was compounded by the postwar baby boom in which a younger population moved to the city. This left an older—and less prosperous—generation to spiritually and financially support the shrines located in the countryside.

With dwindling support for rural shines as the local population aged, shrine festivals were affected as well. Without young families and enthusiastic teenagers to participate in rural celebrations, the once-vibrant *matsuri* of old had, in some cases, become extremely low-key affairs with only a few dozen people in attendance.

Meanwhile, city-based shrines experienced their own problems. In *Shinto and the State, 1868–1988,* Helen Hardacre offers this bleak assessment:

> [Urban] parishes have . . . not succeeded well in integrating new immigrants. Never a democratic organization, the parish offers little attraction to younger [people], who find that they can participate in festivals without taking ongoing responsibility for shrine maintenance, and increasingly this is the tendency. Because Shinto's ties to the state have been so reduced, parish membership no longer offers

either a means of access to the prestige of the state or the opportunities for self-promotion and entrepreneurship seen before 1945.

An important factor contributing to Shinto's postwar decline is the sense that it has been discredited by the loss of World War II, that it has been exposed as bankrupt and as an empty shell in the absence of state patronage. This attitude finds confirmation in the increasingly secular disposition of the society, the growing prestige of science (seen by most as antithetical to religion of any kind), and the media's tendency to ignore or ridicule religion. The efforts of the priesthood to meet these various challenges have been feeble and ineffectual.[80]

To make up for the financial shortfall and lack of public support, Shinto shrines turned to money-making ventures in order to survive. They even opened their halls to events such as nontraditional weddings, parties, and other uses.

Returning to Shinto

Although a majority of people were ambivalent toward their native religion in the sixties and seventies, Shrine Shinto experienced a popular resurgence in the 1980s and 1990s. Business, museums, and other institutions eager to promote Japanese history and culture turned to shrine patronage as a way to improve public relations. Wealthy business leaders became eager to support the shrines, as John K. Nelson writes in *Enduring Identities: The Guise of Shinto in Contemporary Japan:*

> Many of these individuals, socialized and educated during

the prewar period . . . returned to shrines in their moneyed later years as important patrons for maintaining and repairing shrine buildings, funding the staging of major festivals, and permitting shrines to use their business and political networks for fund-raising. In exchange, they are often given what they see as potential access to national status hierarchies connected with the Jinja Honcho, [such as] the imperial household . . . and other elites. A shrine elder in northern Kyoto

Businesspeople visit a shrine. Business leaders often give monetary support to shrines in hopes of improving their business prospects and social status.

said of one wealthy individual, "Whenever we're short of funds, we can always rely on him for a million yen [around $9,000] . . . but it's important not to ask too often." Affiliation with a major shrine [is] often a protective or decorative one, sought by many individuals for self promotion (of one's status, heritage, or lineage) and entrepreneurial gains that extend into business and social networks.[81]

The rebounding popularity of Shinto may also be attributed to a new generation, born after World War II, whose patriotism has not been called into question by the ultranationalism of the past and who are proud of their country's rich ancient heritage. These people see shrine rites and *matsuri* as windows to the past and a way to take part in unique neighborhood events that offer a feeling of community in an increasingly alienated modern world.

The media has played a part in this trend, promoting shrine tourism with programs on television, guidebooks, and articles in newspapers and magazines. As Nelson writes: "A tourist can see a shrine, . . . eat regional delicacies, and shop in nearby boutiques or arcades all in an hour or two."[82]

Visitors to the Kamigamo Shrine

Although more people may be visiting shrines, they are not necessarily aware of the roots of the Shinto religion. In the late 1990s, Nelson surveyed people who visited the popular Kamigamo Shrine (officially named Kamowake Ikazuchi Jinja) in Kyoto. According to a website featuring Nelson's photographs and information about the shrine, the shrine's principle *kami,* named Wake Ikazuchi,

embodies thunder, lightning, and storms, and serves in a dual role: first, as a barrier to protect the imperial capital from all kinds of threats associated with the inauspicious northeast direction, and second, to threaten the court with flooding rivers or excessive rain should the [local] Kamo clan's interests not be adequately accommodated by the [imperial] court.[83]

Kamigamo is second only in popularity to the Grand Shrine at Ise, which is considered the most sacred of all Shinto shrines. The attitudes of visitors, however, illustrate the problems facing Shinto in modern times. People come to Kamigamo

The torii *at Kyoto's Kamigamo Shrine, the second most popular Shinto shrine.*

for a variety of reasons, almost none of them religious. When Nelson surveyed over a hundred individuals as to why they visited Kamigamo, he elicited these responses:

No special reason. . . . It's a famous place. . . . It's recommended as a nice place. . . . It has famous festivals. . . . It's a good place to walk. . . . We were in the area. . . . It's traditional. . . . It's old. . . . We live nearby. . . . Photography. . . . We were having lunch nearby. . . . I asked for blessings for my company. . . .

It's a good place to meet people. . . . I saw it on television.[84]

The Shinto religion was never mentioned by visitors. And the powerful thunder *kami* enshrined at the site was unknown to most. In fact, only 14 percent knew Wake Ikazuchi's name. This discovery, however, did not shock the shrine's senior priest, who said: "I'm amazed . . . that 14 percent were correct. That's much higher than I thought it would be!"[85]

As the priest knew, and Nelson discovered, most visitors to the shrine were interested in the cultural, rather than religious aspects of the site. The shrine precinct's natural environment—a stream, trees, and landscaping—also proved to be a big draw for visitors seeking some solace in the hectic city of Kyoto, home to over 2 million people.

Despite the ambivalence of shrine visitors to Kamigamo, about a third of the visitors to the shrine continue to perform traditional rituals such as offering money, bowing, clapping hands, and reciting silent prayers. Nelson, however, hesitates to ascribe motivations to these pious acts: "Whether they do so because some feel the *kami* is present, because their sense of ritual propriety requires it, or because it is simply an acceptable social form of interaction with the place, I am still reluctant to assert...."[86]

New Concern for Global Problems

While visitors to Kamigamo may be interested in Japan's cultural her-itage, many seem to have more pressing concerns in their daily lives. Shinto leaders realize that this is a problem and have tried to update their religion to be more relevant to modern concerns.

Global problems such as pollution, starvation, and poverty are now affecting people in all countries

One Visitor's Ritual

Most visitors to the Kamigamo Shrine in Kyoto are unfamiliar with the shrine's principle kami *and visit the site for nonreligious reasons. There are still a few, however, who rely on the shrine for spiritual strength and try to stay in touch with the ancient gods even in the twenty-first century. In* Enduring Identities: The Guise of Shinto in Contemporary Japan, *John K. Nelson writes about one man, known only as Mr. H., who spends over two hundred dollars to take the train to Kamigamo from Yokohama once a month in order to appease Wake Ikazuchi, the* kami *of thunder enshrined at Kamigamo. As Mr. H. told Nelson:*

"I believe this *kami* to be great and fearful, largely because I was granted a vision at [the shrine's sacred mountain] shortly before the terrible typhoon of 1991. It was a beautiful day in early August, still and hot, but not sticky like it usually is, and I had gone to the mountain as is my custom. Suddenly, even though there was no wind, the thick growth of trees and vegetation on the southern face of the mountain became agitated, as if moved by a great wind. However, there was no wind at that moment—so how did it happen? The very next day, [a horrible] typhoon ... hit Japan—eventually extending from Kyushu to northern Honshu—causing damage like we haven't had from a single typhoon in years. The *kami* of thunder and lightning gave me a message, and I've been trying to ready myself for the next one ever since. I do *misogi* [purification by flowing water] daily and have formed a group of people in Yokohama to talk, study, and experience this austerity so that we might be closer to the spiritual world."

A Shinto priest offers a prayer at a summit of religious leaders at the United Nations. Modern Shinto leaders strive to address global issues and promote cooperation.

and at all levels of society. How these issues are influencing the Shinto religion are explored on a web page by Naofusa Hirai, a professor emeritus at Kokugakuin University:

Since the Industrial Revolution, advanced countries including Japan have undergone rapid modernization in pursuit of material comforts and convenience. Unfortunately, these efforts have resulted in producing well-known critical global issues. To cope with such issues,

Shinto leaders have begun to be aware of the necessity of international cooperation and mutual aid with other peoples....

Shinto has the following merits for working positively with interfaith dialogue and cooperation.

1. Shinto's notion of kami emphasizes belief in many deities, and its doctrine does not reject other religions, so it is natural for Shinto to pay respect to other religions and objects of worship.

107

2. Within Shinto, it is thought that nature is the place where kami dwell, and we give thanks for the blessings of nature. This attitude toward nature may be of use to religious people considering environmental problems.

3. Within Japan, there is a tradition of carefully preserving and cultivating religions which originate in other countries. Within its boundaries, various religions have practiced cooperation and harmonious coexistence.[87]

To further these goals, Shinto leaders founded the World Conference on Religion and Peace with other religious leaders in 1970. The Association of Shinto Shrines joined with the effort in 1991, adding an International Department to their board in order to "promote international exchange and cooperation."[88]

Another program is the "offer a meal movement" founded by Sectarian Shintoists, who abstain from one meal a month and donate the money saved to their shrine. These funds are collected and used by international relief organizations to help alleviate world hunger. While fasting once a month may cause some discomfort, according to Hirai, those who contribute have said, "At first we thought this was for the sake of others, but actually we noticed this is the way to strengthen our own faith."[89]

New Religions

Without a formal dogma, scriptures, or a charismatic central leader, Shinto religion has been able to reinvent itself to change with the times. Programs like the "offer a meal movement" combine popular Asian concepts such as self-sacrifice for the common good with a brand of Christian charity found in the West. This sort of flexibility has led to the growth of the New Religions movement within Japan since the end of World War II.

There are over two thousand groups in the New Religions movement, many based on the Shinto religion. Although the religions are diverse and hard to categorize, most continue to venerate *kami* and ancestors. Many of the New Religions leave Shinto tradition behind, however, by sponsoring support groups where followers can discuss daily problems with other devotees and learn to improve their lives through harmonious relations with others, hard work, and sincerity.

A large percentage of the New Religions were founded by charismatic leaders, some of them women, who had spiritual awakenings they felt compelled to convey to others. This is often done in small groups, where devotees are encouraged to contact the deities directly and rely on their spiritual faith to heal physical and mental problems.

The PL Kyodan is one sect within the New Religions movement. Often called the "religion of art," PL Kyodan is considered by its 2.6 million adherents to be a Shinto sect. It promotes individualism and self-expression, concepts abhorrent to leaders of State Shinto earlier in the century.

The movement gained popularity after 1945 as Japanese people were able to express themselves openly without condemnation by government or religious authorities. Today PL Kyodan, with its motto "Life is Art," has a divine law containing twenty-one "precepts for life," some of which appear to be outside the orthodox Shinto thought of Japan's premodern period. These concepts include the following:

The whole life of the individual is a continuous succession of self-expressions.

The individual is a manifestation of God.

We suffer if we do not manifest ourselves.

We lose ourselves if we are swayed by our feelings. . . .

Practice at once whatever our first inspiration dictates. . . .

Live in Perfect Liberty.

Other PL Kyodan precepts suggest connections with classical Shinto, and others might be considered to be extensions of Shinto thought:

All things exist in mutual relation to one another.

Live radiantly as the sun.

All men are equal.

Bring mutual happiness through our expressions. . . .

All things exist for world peace.

Our whole environment is the mirror of our mind.

All things make progress and develop.

Grasp the heart of everything.

At every moment man stands at the crossroad of good and evil. . . .

Attain the perfect harmonious state of mind and matter.[90]

The New Religions movement shows the flexibility of Shinto in the modern age. After a damaging war in which Shinto was used for ultra-nationalistic purposes, dozens of Shinto sects such as PL Kyodan were formed to advocate world peace, art, beauty, and freedom from materialism. With its historic roots in tolerance and acceptance of other religions, Shinto has been able to change with the times in order to fulfill the needs of its followers.

New Attitudes in a New Era

While the popularity of Shinto has fallen and risen in the postwar years, it still remains vital to the Japanese culture and character. Over 80 million people continue to visit Shinto shrines on important

People walk down a Kobe street lined with buildings destroyed by the 1995 earthquake, just one of the many difficulties to hit Japan in recent decades.

national holidays such as the New Year's celebrations, and the precincts remain popular tourist destinations for travelers. In fact, the popularity of Shinto seems to be growing again as Japan has suffered physically and financially in recent years.

Beginning in the late 1980s, Japan suffered a series of national setbacks that saw people turning to Shinto for comfort. As Nelson writes:

If anything, the Japanese today are searching for answers and directions like never before. The passing of the emperor [Hirohito], delinquency and violence in Japan's lauded educational system, a series of corruption scandals among politicians, terrorism within Japan, rising unemployment—the list could go on. In each case, fundamental assumptions about the order and stability of social life in Japan have been shaken and dislodged. And if socially related turmoil wasn't enough, the Kobe earthquake in 1995 (in which over five thousand people died in an area thought safe) added a harsh, physical dimension to the rush of paradigm-shifting events. After two decades of economic growth and relative political stability, citizens were now forced to confront what it means to be Japanese in a land where change and uncertainty are as much a part of social realities as they are of geological instabilities.

In times like these, precedent has shown that people frequently turn to religion. One might suppose that Buddhism would enter the picture, with its existentially soothing philosophies of impermanence and transience. But as these situations and incidents played out in the early 1990s, the Japanese were less enamored with Buddhist philosophy than with their other, and older, tradition of reassurance: Shinto. While cultural and religious trends come and go, shrine Shinto remains one of the most long-lived of all Japan's institutions, largely because (after nearly fourteen centuries) it continues to help form, orient, and empower a sense of local and ethnic identity. Still relevant in the shaping of contemporary cultural identity as well, Shinto's social presence—amplified by seasonal festivals, the influences they have on communal dynamics, as well as the rituals provided by local shrines to mark life transitions and manage anxieties—is an institution that is "culturally loud."[91]

Perhaps paradoxically, modern-day Japanese culture remains steeped in ancient Shinto traditions formu-

Shinto and Modern Technology

Even as Japan has become a high-tech leader in science and industry, the Shinto religion remains a part of everyday life even in the innermost circles of scientific research, as John K. Nelson writes in Enduring Identities: The Guise of Shinto in Contemporary Japan:

"In 1970 scientists and administrators of Japan's Space Development Agency were ready to launch the country's first satellite. Under great pressure to succeed and thus further demonstrate to the world Japan's continuing postwar recovery, they carried out their plans meticulously. Then they took one final precaution. Shortly before the launch, senior representatives of the agency visited Chichibu Shinto shrine located near Tokyo. Their goal: to petition its deity Myoken (the North Star) that their endeavor might succeed. When the rocket blasted off and placed a satellite in its intended orbit, these same individuals made a return trip to express their gratitude before moving on to other projects. . . .

[Unlike] their Western counterparts, Japanese rocket scientists see no opposition between their physics and computations, and the spirits of powerful deities *(kami)* that animate life, influence physical phenomenon, and enhance creativity. . . .

Consider the following further examples: one of the world's most powerful electron microscopes (at Osaka University) until recently had a Shinto amulet attached to it; Japan's first and highly controversial nuclear waste repository was dedicated by a Shinto priest waving a purificatory wand over the site in 1992; after a small shrine was relocated for a runway expansion project at Narita International Airport, one of its *torii* gateways remained for years because local people feared reprisals from the shrine's agitated deities. . . . Many companies and corporations continue to venerate in-house shrines whose deities include the company's founder, are specific to the geographical place of business, or are related to the product in some way."

Though modern Japanese culture is dramatically different from the agricultural society that gave birth to Shinto, the religion remains a vital part of Japanese life.

lated in an agricultural society nearly two millennia ago. Yet it is Shinto's teachings about spiritual and physical purity as well as respect for community, family, and the ubiquitous *kami* that form the building blocks of today's successful Japanese society.

Notes

Introduction: The Shinto Religion

1. Gorazd Vihar and Charlotte Anderson, *Matsuri: World of Japanese Festivals*. Tokyo: Shufunotomo, 1994, p. 6.
2. B. A. Robinson, "Shinto," July 7, 1999. www.religioustolerance. org/shinto.htm.
3. C. Scott Littleton, *Eastern Wisdom*. New York: Henry Holt, 1996, p. 144.
4. Beth Reiber, *Tokyo*. New York: Macmillan Travel, 1998, pp. 11–12.
5. Jean Herbert, *Shinto: At the Fountainhead of Japan*. New York: Stein and Day, 1967, p. 21.

Chapter 1: The Historic Roots of Shinto

6. Robinson, "Shinto."
7. Quoted in R. H. P. Mason and J. G. Caiger, *A History of Japan*. Rutland, VT: Charles E. Tuttle, 1997, p. 33.
8. Donald Philippi, *Norito: A New Translation of the Ancient Japanese Ritual Prayers*. Tokyo: Institute for Japanese Culture and Classics, Kokugakuin University, 1959, p. 47.
9. Quoted in Mason and Caiger, *History of Japan*, p. 33.
10. Marion May Dilts, *The Pageant of Japanese History*. New York: Longmans, Green, 1961, p. 15.
11. Schauwecker's Guide to Japan, "Japanese Buddhism," 1996–2000. www.japan-guide.com/e/e2055. html.
12. W. G. Aston, trans., *Nihongi: Chronicles of Japan from the Earliest Times to A.D. 697*. London: George Allen & Unwin, 1956, p. 66.
13. Quoted in Post Wheeler, ed., *The Sacred Scriptures of the Japanese*. New York: Henry Shuman, 1952, p. xvii.
14. Wheeler, *Sacred Scriptures*, p. xvii.
15. Sokyo Ono, *Shinto and the Kami Way*. Rutland, VT: Charles E. Tuttle, 1962, p. 10.
16. Stuart D. B. Picken, *Essentials of Shinto*. Westport, CT: Greenwood Press, 1994, p. 15.
17. Jack Finegan, *Archeology of World Religions*. Princeton, NJ: Princeton University Press, 1952, p. 445.
18. Quoted in Picken, *Essentials of Shinto*, p. 16.
19. Translated in Finegan, *Archeology of World Religions*, p. 447.
20. Picken, *Essentials of Shinto*, p. 23.
21. Picken, *Essentials of Shinto*, p. 33.
22. Mason and Caiger, *History of Japan*, p. 296.
23. "Emperor System (State Shinto)," Overview of World Religions, 1999. http://philtar.ucsm.ac.uk/encyclopedia/ shinto/state.html.

Chapter 2: Lessons of the *Kami*

24. Ono, *Shinto and the Kami Way*, p. 3.
25. Donald Philippi, trans., *Kojiki*. Tokyo: University of Tokyo Press, 1968, p. 49.
26. Quoted in Wheeler, *Sacred Scriptures*, p. 6.
27. Picken, *Essentials of Shinto*, p. 62.
28. Vihar and Anderson, *Matsuri*, p. 6.
29. Littleton, *Eastern Wisdom*, pp. 149–50.
30. Picken, *Essentials of Shinto*, p. 64.
31. Herbert, *Shinto*, p. 59.
32. Herbert, *Shinto*, p. 60.
33. Robinson, "Shinto."
34. Naofusa Hirai, "Shinto: A Portrait." www.silcom.com/~origin/sbcr/sbcr131.
35. Ono, *Shinto and the Kami Way*, p. 103.
36. Quoted in H. Byron Earhart, ed., *Religion in the Japanese Experience*. Encino, CA: Dickenson Publishing, 1974, p. 147.
37. Hirai, "Shinto."
38. Littleton, *Eastern Wisdom*, p. 155.
39. Quoted in Earhart, *Religion in the Japanese Experience*, p. 150.
40. Quoted in Earhart, *Religion in the Japanese Experience*, p. 150.
41. Quoted in Earhart, *Religion in the Japanese Experience*, p. 151.
42. Herbert, *Shinto*, p. 155.
43. Quoted in Herbert, *Shinto*, p. 157.
44. Herbert Plutschow, *Matsuri: The Festivals of Japan*. Surrey, Eng.: Japan Library, 1996, p. 72.
45. Plutschow, *Matsuri*, pp. 72–73.
46. Picken, *Essentials of Shinto*, p. 171.
47. Herbert, *Shinto*, p. 80.

Chapter 3: Shrines and Priests

48. Littleton, *Eastern Wisdom*, p. 151.
49. Ono, *Shinto and the Kami Way*, p. 28.
50. Herbert, *Shinto*, p. 94.
51. Ono, *Shinto and the Kami Way*, pp. 27–28.
52. Picken, *Essentials of Shinto*, p. 93.
53. Herbert, *Shinto*, p. 119.
54. Quoted in Ono, *Shinto and the Kami Way*, p. 23.
55. Ono, *Shinto and the Kami Way*, p. 25.
56. Ono, *Shinto and the Kami Way*, p. 60.
57. Herbert, *Shinto*, p. 155.
58. Picken, *Essentials of Shinto*, p. 165.
59. Ono, *Shinto and the Kami Way*, pp. 61–62.
60. Ono, *Shinto and the Kami Way*, p. 42.
61. Picken, *Essentials of Shinto*, p. 191.
62. Ono, *Shinto and the Kami Way*, p. 97.

Chapter 4: Ceremonies and Celebrations

63. Herbert, *Shinto*, p. 166.
64. Herbert, *Shinto*, p. 166.
65. Vihar and Anderson, *Matsuri: World of Japanese Festivals*, p. 5.
66. Picken, *Essentials of Shinto*, p. 177.
67. Vihar and Anderson, *Matsuri*, p. 13.
68. Quoted in Plutschow, *Matsuri*, pp. 44–45.
69. Shinto Online Network Association,

"The Jinja Shinto: Festivals." www.jinja.or.jp/english/s-4e.html.

70. Plutschow, *Matsuri*, pp. 90–91.

71. Picken, *Essentials of Shinto*, p. 181.

72. Annual Ceremonies at the Kasama Inari Jinja. www.kasama.or.jp/english/gyoji/.

73. Shinto Online Network Association, "Folk Shinto: The Yearly Round of Observances." www.jinja.or.jp/english/s-3a.html.

74. Shinto Online Network Association, "Procedures of a Worshipping Rite." www.jinja.or.jp/english/s-4d.html.

75. Vihar and Anderson, *Matsuri*, p. 13.

Chapter 5: Shinto in the Modern World

76. Quoted in Helen Hardacre, *Shinto and the State, 1868-1988*. Princeton, NJ: Princeton University Press, 1989, p. 167.

77. Quoted in "Japan-Constitution," ICL-Japan-Constitution, February 17, 2001. www.uni-wuerzburg.de/law/ja00000_.html.

78. Jinja Honcho (Association of Shinto Shrines). www.jinjahoncho.or.jp/en/h_top.html.

79. Ken Watanabe, "The Emperor of Japan and the History of the Imperial Household of Japan," 1998–2000. www.geocities.com/~watanabe_ken/tenno.html#gendi.

80. Hardacre, *Shinto and the State*, p. 142.

81. John K. Nelson, *Enduring Identities: The Guise of Shinto in Contemporary Japan*. Honolulu: University of Hawaii Press, 2000, p. 129.

82. Nelson, *Enduring Identities*, p. 130.

83. John K. Nelson, "Kamigamo Shrine Map," Shinto Slide Show, 1999. http://ecai.berkeley.edu/shinto/slide.html.

84. Nelson, *Enduring Identities*, p. 30.

85. Quoted in Nelson, *Enduring Identities*, p. 30.

86. Nelson, *Enduring Identities*, p. 41.

87. Hirai, "Shinto."

88. Hirai, "Shinto."

89. Quoted in Hirai, "Shinto."

90. Quoted in Picken, *Essentials of Shinto*, pp. 276–77.

91. Nelson, *Enduring Identities*, pp. 2–3.

For Further Reading

Paula R. Hartz, *Shinto*. New York: Facts On File, 1997. From the World Religions series, this book covers the development of Shinto from prehistory to modern times.

Don Nardo, *Traditional Japan*. San Diego: Lucent Books, 1995. Examines the history and culture of Japan until the Meiji Restoration in 1868.

Patricia D. Netzley, *Japan*. San Diego: Lucent Books, 2000. Examines the land, people, history, politics, and culture of Japan.

Sokyo Ono, *Shinto and the Kami Way*. Rutland, VT: Charles E. Tuttle, 1962. A simple yet definitive book on the Shinto religion written by a professor at the Shinto university Kokugakuin Daigaku. The author is also a lecturer for the Japanese Association of Shinto Shrines and executive director of the Japan Religious Co-operative Council.

Donald L. Philippi, ed., *Norito*. Princeton, NJ: Princeton University Press, 1990. One of the few books available with English translations of beautiful Shinto *norito*, or poetic religious prayers.

Julia Piggott, *Japanese Mythology*. New York: Peter Bedrick Books, 1983. A colorful book with dozens of fascinating Shinto stories, legends, myths, and monsters along with scores of pictures of Japanese shrines, paintings, masks, and other artwork. The author has written several books about Japanese mythology and descends from a family of English diplomats and statesmen who served in Japan.

Ian Reader, *Simple Guide to Shinto, The Religion of Japan*. Honolulu: University of Hawaii Press, 1998. Part of the Simple Guides to World Religions series, this book offers basic information about Shinto.

Earle Rice Jr., *Kamikazes*. San Diego: Lucent Books, 2000. Examines the events and personalities that were instrumental in Japan's adoption of *kamikaze*, or suicide, missions in the later stages of World War II.

Gorazd Vihar and Charlotte Anderson, *Matsuri: World of Japanese Festivals*. Tokyo: Shufunotomo, 1994. A beautiful book with a short introduction about Shinto and hundreds of color photographs of *matsuri* festivals in which worshipers don elaborate costumes and masks to sing and dance in honor of *kami* spirits.

Works Consulted

W. G. Aston, trans., *Nihongi: Chronicles of Japan from the Earliest Times to A.D. 697.* London: George Allen & Unwin, 1956. A translation of the history of ancient Japan that was first published in 720 A.D., detailing the traditions of the Shinto religion and *kami* deities from ancient times.

Marion May Dilts, *The Pageant of Japanese History.* New York: Longmans, Green, 1961. A book first published before World War II that covers the earliest settlers of Japan and explores Japan's ruling dynasties, art, and culture.

H. Byron Earhart, ed., *Religion in the Japanese Experience.* Encino, CA: Dickenson Publishing, 1974. A collection of essays about religions in ancient and modern Japan including Shinto, Buddhism, Taoism, Chris-tianity, and others.

Jack Finegan, *Archeology of World Religions.* Princeton, NJ: Princeton University Press, 1952. A book that uses archaeology as a basis to describe the roots of religions such as Hinduism, Islam, and Shinto, employing ancient documents, architecture, pottery, and artwork.

Helen Hardacre, *Shinto and the State, 1868–1988.* Princeton, NJ: Princeton University Press, 1989. Detailed study of State Shinto as it was practiced in Japan from the time of the Meiji Restoration in 1868 until the book was published in the late 1980s.

Jean Herbert, *Shinto: At the Fountainhead of Japan.* New York: Stein and Day, 1967. An exhaustive study of Shinto written by a professor of Asian religion, philosophy, and mythology who compiled the material in the volume for over thirty years.

C. Scott Littleton, *Eastern Wisdom.* New York: Henry Holt, 1996. An illustrated guide to the religions and philosophies of the East, including Shinto, Hindu, Buddhism, and others.

R. H. P. Mason and J. G. Caiger, *A History of Japan.* Rutland, VT: Charles E. Tuttle, 1997. Comprehensive book on Japanese civilization and culture from ancient times until the present with an in-depth analysis of religion, culture, and the arts.

John K. Nelson, *Enduring Identities: The Guise of Shinto in Contemporary Japan.* Honolulu: University of Hawaii Press, 2000. A scholarly study of Shinto's lasting relevance in modern Japanese culture written by an anthropology and religion professor at the University of Texas.

Donald Philippi, trans., *Kojiki.* Tokyo: University of Tokyo Press, 1968. The modern translation of the "Records of Ancient Matters," which details the legends, narratives, songs, anecdotes, and imperial genealogy of the Shinto religion.

Donald Philippi, *Norito: A New Translation of the Ancient Japanese Ritual Prayers*. Tokyo: Institute for Japanese Culture and Classics, Kokugakuin University, 1959. A book with detailed translations of *norito*, ancient Shinto prayers.

Stuart D. B. Picken, *Essentials of Shinto*. Westport, CT: Greenwood Press, 1994. A thorough exploration of Shinto from ancient times to the modern era written by a professor of philosophy at International Christian University in Tokyo.

Herbert Plutschow, *Matsuri: The Festivals of Japan*. Surrey, Eng.: Japan Library, 1996. A scholarly work that explores the physical and metaphysical aspects of the *matsuri* festivals of Japan in great detail.

Beth Reiber, *Tokyo*. New York: Macmillan Travel, 1998. A Frommer's travel book about Tokyo with chapters concerning religion, history, planning a trip, restaurants, accommodations, and other information important to a traveler.

Post Wheeler, ed., *The Sacred Scriptures of the Japanese*. New York: Henry Shuman, 1952. A complete presentation of the sacred *Kojiki* and *Nihongi*, the first written works of Shinto and Japanese history, respectively.

Internet Sources

Annual Ceremonies at the Kasama Inari Jinja. www.kasama.or.jp/english/gyoji/. A website sponsored by the Shrine Offices of Kasama Inari Jinja that details the religious significance of several important Shinto holidays.

Basic Terms of Shinto. www.kokugakuin. ac.jp/ijcc/wp/bts/index.html. Hosted by the Institute for Japanese Culture and Classics at Kokugakuin University, this website allows users to type in common Shinto words and phrases and defines them in English.

Electric Samurai Asian Network, Cyber Shrine. www.kiku.com/electric_ samurai/cyber_shrine/. A website with dozens of photos of awe-inspiring shrines located throughout Japan. There are also about a half-dozen shrines represented with QuickTime movies that allow viewers to virtually tour the precincts in a 360-degree sweep.

Naofusa Hirai, "Shinto: A Portrait." www.silcom.com/~origin/sbcr/sbcr131. A site with a short explanation of Shinto beliefs by a professor emeritus at Kokugakuin University, Tokyo, with assistance from Professor H. Byron Earhart of Western Michigan University.

ICL-Japan-Constitution, "Japan-Constitution," February 17, 2001. www.uni-wuerzburg.de/law/ja00000_.html. A website that lists the constitutional documents and country information for more than eighty countries around the world.

Yoko Inoue, "Hinamatsuri—March Girl's Festival," 1999, www.aboutbbs.com/yuria/hinamatsuri/. A website that lists the details of the Japanese festival Hinamatsuri, also known as Girls' Day or the Doll Festival.

Institute for Japanese Culture and Classics, "Basic Terms of Shinto," 1997. www.kokugakuin.ac.jp/ijcc/wp/bts/. A search engine that offers definitions of Shinto terms entered by user.

International Shinto Foundation, "What Is Shinto." http://shinto.org/menu-e.html. A short description of the Shinto religion.

Jinja Honcho (Association of Shinto Shrines). www.jinjahoncho.or.jp/en/h_top.html. A website run by the organization that oversees the administration of Japan's eighty-one thousand Shinto shrines.

Rick Kennedy, *Tokyo Q Magazine*, 1995–1999. 202.221.249.1/tokyoq/index.html. A site maintained by *Tokyo Q*, an on-line arts and entertainment magazine edited by Kennedy, an author of the travel book *Little Adventures in Tokyo*. Kennedy's warmhearted observations of Tokyo culture through Western eyes are amusing, entertaining, and educational.

John K. Nelson, "Kamigamo Shrine Map," Shinto Slide Show, 1999. http://ecai.berkeley.edu/shinto/slide.html. A site with excellent pictures relating to Shinto shrines, festivals, and practices with a special focus on the popular Kamigamo Shrine in Kyoto.

Overview of World Religions, "Emperor System (State Shinto)," 1999. http://philtar.ucsm.ac.uk/encyclopedia/shinto/state.html. A website run by the Religion and Ethics Department at St. Martin's College in England that details the history and philosophy of Shinto, its many denominations, and other world religions.

B. A. Robinson, "Shinto," July 7, 1999. www.religioustolerance.org/shinto.htm. A detailed description of Shinto covering history, beliefs, practices, forms of Shinto, texts, numbers of adherents, and links to other Shinto sites, some written in Japanese.

Vimalin Rujivacharakul and Michele Delattre, "Sacred Spaces of Shinto." www.ias.berkeley.edu/orias/visuals/japan_visuals/shintoB.HTM. A beautifully designed website dedicated to teaching religion through art and architecture with pictures of Shinto shrines along with detailed explanations of the meaning behind the various structures.

Schauwecker's Guide to Japan, "Japanese Buddhism," 1996–2000. www.japan-guide.com/e/e2055.
html. A website that explores the arts, news, entertainment, history, language, politics, religions, sports, and other institutions of Japan. Also includes historic photos, Japanese-oriented chat rooms, and commercial links.

Shinto Online Network Association. www.jinja.or.jp/english/index.html.
According to their website, they are a "non-profit volunteer organization with the objective of publicizing Japanese tradition and a correct understanding of the Shinto religion . . . run by volunteer Shinto priests."

Ken Watanabe, "The Emperor of Japan and the History of the Imperial Household of Japan," 1998–2000. www.geocities.com/~watanabe_ken/tenno.html#gendi.

Index

Picture Credits

About the Author

Stuart A. Kallen is the author of more than 150 nonfiction books for children and young adults. He has written on topics ranging from the theory of relativity to rock-and-roll history to life on the American frontier. In addition, Mr. Kallen has written award-winning children's videos and television scripts. In his spare time, Stuart A. Kallen is a singer/song-writer/guitarist in San Diego, California.